# With One Voice

# With One Voice

*Translation and Implementation of the Third Edition of the* Roman Missal

FEDERATION OF DIOCESAN LITURGICAL COMMISSIONS
Washington, D.C.

# Contents

# Foreword

O ne of the most often quoted teachings of the Second Vatican Council comes from *Sacrosanctum Concilium*, the *Constitution on the Sacred Liturgy*, reminding the Church of the central place of the liturgy in the life of the Church:

> The liturgy is the summit toward which the activity of the Church is directed; at the same time it is the fount from which all the Church's power flows. For the aim and object of apostolic works is that all who are made children of God by faith and baptism should come together to praise God in the midst of his Church, to take part in the sacrifice, and to eat the Lord's Supper.
>
> The liturgy in its turn moves the faithful, filled with "the paschal sacraments," to be "one in holiness" [Prayer After Communion, Easter Vigil]; it prays that "they may hold fast in their lives to what they have grasped by their faith" [Opening Prayer, Mass for Monday of Easter Week]; the renewal in the eucharist of the covenant between the Lord and his people draws the faithful into the compelling love of Christ and sets them on fire.[1]

The lived experience of the Church gives witness to this fact. Indeed, for most Catholics, the Sunday liturgy is the heart of the Church.

In the years leading up to the observance of the Great Jubilee Year 2000, Servant of God Pope John Paul II called the Church to a collective "examination of conscience," to include its own practices with regard to the Sunday Eucharist.[2] At the close of the Great Jubilee, Pope John Paul wrote: "In the twentieth century, especially since the Council, there has been a great development in the way the Christian community celebrates the Sacraments, especially the Eucharist. It is necessary to continue in this direction, and to stress

---

1    Second Vatican Council, *Sacrosanctum Concilium* (SC), no. 10, in *Documents on the Liturgy, 1963-1979: Conciliar, Papal, and Curial Texts* (DOL), trans. and ed. International Commission on English in the Liturgy (ICEL) (Collegeville, MN: The Liturgical Press, 1982). Henceforth, citations from the DOL will include a reference number from the DOL.

2    Pope John Paul II, Apostolic letter *Tertio Millennio Adveniente* (*On the Coming of the Third Millennium*) (Washington, DC: United States Conference of Catholic Bishops, 1994), no. 6.

particularly *the Sunday Eucharist* and *Sunday* itself experienced as a special day of faith, the day of the Risen Lord and of the gift of the Spirit, the true weekly Easter."[3] To this end, Pope John Paul promulgated the *Missale Romanum, editio typica tertia*, in 2000. That text was published in 2002, and for several years since, the work of preparing translations of the *Roman Missal* into vernacular languages has been ongoing.

This collection of essays, commissioned by the Federation of Diocesan Liturgical Commissions, provides a strong foundation to prepare for the reception and implementation of the third edition of the *Roman Missal*. The bishops' Committee on Divine Worship of the United States Conference of Catholic Bishops (USCCB) has outlined a process of catechesis as we work toward the implementation of the new *Missal*. Not only should pastors and other leaders provide the necessary training and teaching about the changes in the texts, but this time of transition affords a great opportunity to examine and reflect on the nature and importance of the Eucharist in the life of the Church. In this way, both pastors and the faithful can deepen their awareness of the importance of their own "full, conscious, and active participation"[4] in the liturgy and thus deepen their communion with the Risen Lord.

The implementation of the third edition of the *Roman Missal* will be a time of great challenge for many people. The liturgical texts we have known so well and have used effectively in the celebration of the Mass are changing. The way in which the liturgy is celebrated within the Church grows and evolves with the Church. The substance of the liturgy, however, is always the same: it is the same Lord Jesus Christ who is the real celebrant, who is present to his Church, who feeds us with his own Body and Blood. The essay by Bishop Gerald Kicanas offers an honest and helpful perspective on embracing change within the context of the liturgical history of the Church. He encourages leadership at all levels of the Church in the United States, in each diocese, and in every parish to accept the challenge to facilitate the transition to the new *Missal*. Fr. John Foster

---

3     Pope John Paul II, Apostolic letter *Novo Millennio Ineunte* (*At the Close of the Great Jubilee of the Year 2000*), no. 35, *www.vatican.va/holy_father/john_paul_ii/apost_letters/documents/hf_jp-ii_apl_20010106_novo-millennio-ineunte_en.html.*

4     SC, no. 14 (DOL 14).

breaks down the particular roles and responsibilities of bishops and pastors regarding catechesis and the celebration of the liturgy.

With the challenges of leadership in a time of change as a backdrop, foundational background on the liturgy is provided in essays by Fr. Mark Francis, CSV, and Fr. Paul Turner. They place this particular moment in the history of the liturgy within the broader context of the life of the Church. Fr. Francis reflects on the importance of the active participation of the faithful in the liturgy, and he invites all of us to renew our own commitment to encourage one another to participate not just fully and actively, but *consciously*—to celebrate the liturgy with a thorough understanding of what we do. Fr. Turner explores the detailed process of translation and sheds light on the challenges faced by those involved in producing the text that we now prepare to introduce. Such background helps us to appreciate all the more the rich heritage of the liturgical tradition of the Church, which emphasizes the truth of the axiom *lex orandi, lex credendi*: that what we believe is expressed and articulated in how we pray and worship.

I am grateful to the Federation of Diocesan Liturgical Commissions for undertaking the task of providing resources to aid in catechetical efforts in preparation for the implementation of the third edition of the *Roman Missal*. The members, the board, and the staff of the Federation have demonstrated great zeal in committing themselves to the work that lies before us: to prepare and support the clergy and other leaders and the faithful to celebrate the liturgy prayerfully, reverently, effectively, and faithfully as it is handed down from one generation to the next within the Church. May the Lord bless us as we undertake this effort to celebrate the sacred liturgy with greater fervor and deeper devotion.

Most Reverend Arthur J. Serratelli
Bishop of Paterson
Chair, USCCB Committee on Divine Worship

# With One Voice

# CHAPTER 1

# Liturgical Leadership in a Time of Change

MOST REVEREND GERALD F. KICANAS, BISHOP OF TUCSON

C hange happens. Just take a look at your grade school picture; you will know what I mean. Change happens throughout the span of our lives. We change in appearance. We change in interests. We change in behavior. Change happens. History records changes that have taken place in every society, in every culture, in every organization.

Some changes mark progress. Horse-driven carriages have given way to combustion-engine cars. Combustion-engine cars are giving way to hybrids. Typewriters succumbed to the emergence of the computer. The photocopier replaced the messy stencils on the mimeograph machine. Fax and e-mail have lessened our reliance on post offices.

Some changes mark decline. Regimes collapse, businesses fold, stock portfolios fall, homes are lost, and churches close. Change characterizes all life, personal and organizational.

Change was the slogan of Barack Obama's presidential campaign in 2008. Posters, buttons, bumper stickers, and T-shirts bore the words "Change you can believe in." The message promoted the idea that things could be different and better. His election marked a momentous change: for the first time, an African American is president of the United States.

Change happens.

# LITURGICAL CHANGE

Change happens in the Church as well. This should not surprise us. While the Magisterium keeps the Church in continuity with the intentions of its founder, Jesus Christ, the Church as a living institution changes. Throughout the Church's history, liturgical changes have taken place—some significant, some minor, some grand, some very simple.

Pope Benedict XVI, in his post-synodal exhortation *Sacramentum caritatis*, traces the course of change in liturgy:

> If we consider the bimillenary history of God's Church, guided by the wisdom of the Holy Spirit, we can gratefully admire the orderly development of the ritual forms in which we commemorate the event of our salvation. From the varied forms of the early centuries, still resplendent in the rites of the Ancient Churches of the East, up to the spread of the Roman rite; from the clear indications of the Council of Trent and the Missal of Saint Pius V to the liturgical renewal called for by the Second Vatican Council: in every age of the Church's history the eucharistic celebration, as the source and summit of her life and mission, shines forth in the liturgical rite in all its richness and variety.[1]

Consider what has taken place in the liturgy in our own lifetimes since the Second Vatican Council's promulgation of *Sacrosanctum Concilium* (*Constitution on the Sacred Liturgy*) in 1963. The priest now faces the community. We pray in the vernacular. People participate in a full and conscious way. Laity serve as lectors and extraordinary ministers of holy communion, as cantors and psalmists.

For some time now, the International Commission on English in the Liturgy (ICEL) and the bishops' conferences of English-speaking countries have been working on an English translation of the third edition of the *Missale Romanum*, which was promulgated in 2000 by Pope John Paul II and published in Latin. The task of translating the *Missale Romanum* into English has been painstaking work; after all, something as sacred as the texts of our prayer cannot be dealt with lightly.

The translation has now received the *recognitio* by the Holy See. Now the translation will come into use, and the community

---

1    Pope Benedict XVI, Post-synodal apostolic exhortation *Sacramentum caritatis* (SacCar) (Washington, DC: United States Conference of Catholic Bishops [USCCB], 2007), no. 3.

will again experience change in the celebration of the Eucharist. The celebrant and the community will hear and pray different words. We will experience some minor but real changes in the celebration of the liturgy.

In this study paper, I would like to reflect on what has been learned from social science about change and how it can best be managed. I consider the difficulties in accepting change and what they mean for the upcoming liturgical changes. I then focus on the areas in which I believe critical change needs to happen as the new English translation is implemented. I discuss the importance of planning for change and engaging in a process to help people understand the content, reasons, and hoped-for results of change. I discuss the role of leadership in change and examine what deters us in dioceses and parishes from managing change well. Finally, I lay out a process that might guide communities of faith in managing the upcoming change in the liturgy with positive results.

Change happens. It is inevitable. Sometimes change is a return to where we were; other times it moves us in a new direction. Any change may have positive or negative results, depending on how that change is led and managed.

# DEALING WITH CHANGE

Organizational development offers insights and directions for leading our way through change. It teaches us that change is always messy, fraught with challenges. Change takes an emotional toll, evokes different and oftentimes idiosyncratic responses from people, and can disrupt and divide a community.[2]

Change can leave an individual or an organization better or worse depending on how that change is prepared for and dealt with. It takes leadership to provide vision and guide an institution through change.

John Kotter, in his book *Leading Change*,[3] suggests that change fails when an organization is complacent, stuck in what it has always done. Change fails when the leader is not engaged or when that leader does not draw in key people to join the team, to get on board. Change fails when it is not clear why a change is happening. There

---

2   See Gerard Egan, *Working the Shadow Side: A Guide to Positive Behind-the-Scenes Management* (San Francisco: Jossey-Bass, Inc., 1994).

3   See John Kotter, *Leading Change* (Boston: Harvard Business School Press, 1996).

is no vision or direction; the change seems aimless and meaningless. Change fails when it is not communicated well in both words and deeds. People need to understand why changes are being made and become convinced of the change's wisdom.

First let us consider the challenges people face in accepting change. Change comes with difficulty, sometimes with resistance, oftentimes with a sense of loss.

Resistance and a sense of loss were certainly the felt experience of some after the momentous changes in liturgy after Vatican II. Some people neither understood nor accepted the changes that were put into effect. In many places the changes happened overnight, with little or no preparation. That was a great mistake. Where and how one prays is sacred to people, affecting us at our deepest roots.

As happens often in many institutions, those affected by the change in liturgy were, too often, not given a full understanding of the reasons for the change nor given the time to allow the major transformation to take hold in the community.

It is no wonder that some, even after so many years, have yet to accept what happened at Vatican II. They sense that something fundamental was lost. They seek to go back to how we celebrated the Mass before Vatican II. Some even continue to reject Vatican II and the changes it brought.

Complicating things in many areas at the time of Vatican II was the fading away of the Catholic neighborhood with the great support that it gave to Catholic practice. Surely this had an effect on how people reacted to the changes of Vatican II.

As we look to the reception of a new *Roman Missal*, what can be done in the United States Conference of Catholic Bishops (USCCB) and within our dioceses and our parishes to facilitate that change so that it does not result in confusion or further division and alienation?

We have already heard comments: "Why are we changing?" "If it is not broken, don't try to fix it." "The new translations are stilted, cumbersome, and unable to be proclaimed." "We do not speak that way in the United States." "I prefer 'and also with you' instead of 'and with your spirit.'"

# CHANGE PROCESS

William Bridges, a noted author on leading people through transitions in organizations and in individuals' lives,[4] speaks of a threefold process involved in accepting change. While change is situational, something new is happening. Transition is psychological, as people and organizations come to terms with those new circumstances.

The first phase is letting go, ending, losing something. As organizations and individuals change, they have to first let go of what was, deal with the loss of what they knew. This phase cannot be ignored. People need time for some grieving.

The second phase is an in-between time, a "neutral zone," a period of adjustment from what was to what is. One is not yet at home with the changes. There is a time of uncertainty, of doubt, of wonderment. Is the new helpful? Is the new better? Is the new an enhancement? People need time to grow familiar with the change, to develop comfort. It is that space between letting go of the first trapeze and grabbing the new trapeze. People feel vulnerable; they have lost something, but they have not yet let the change take hold. This phase, too, is critical and cannot be passed over.

The third phase is the new beginning. In this phase people become comfortable with the change—they come to value and appreciate the change and to see it as helpful, an improvement from what was. We get there only after the first two phases.

# DEALING WITH LITURGICAL CHANGE

The change process starts with an ending and concludes with a beginning. Now that the translation of the *Missale Romanum* is complete and has been granted a *recognitio* from Rome, and as we begin to use it in parish liturgy, we can expect that our communities will move through various stages not unlike what happens in other areas of life affected by change.[5]

Any change in something as fundamental and important as liturgy is met first by surprise and shock. People say, "The changes are

---

4   See William Bridges's books *Managing Transitions* (Cambridge, MA: Da Capo Press, 2003) and *The Way of Transition* (Cambridge, MA: Da Capo Press, 2001).

5   For further reading on this process, see Oliver Recklies, "Managing Change: Definition and Phases in Change Processes," *www.themanager.org/strategy/change_phases.htm*, August 2001.

not necessary." This is followed by denial and refusal. Priests decide to keep celebrating liturgy as they did before the changes, or they make up prayers when they do not like the translation given. The celebration could become "my Mass," not the liturgy of the Church.

This describes what Bridges defines as the first stage of transition: ending, losing, letting go. We ought to expect this and not be surprised by it. We need to give people time to question and grieve.

If we are going to help priests and people move from shock and refusal to acceptance and integration, our communities will need to manage the coming changes effectively. This will take planning and sensitive implementation. It will involve a process in which people are led through what is changing, why it is changing, and how the changes will enhance our celebration of the liturgy.

One challenge that arises in dealing with liturgical change is that such changes do not come from the pews or priests but rather are set down, not chosen; they are handed over, not decided.

This reality, of course, flows from our understanding of the Magisterium and its role in safeguarding the prayer of the Church. Change in liturgical texts cannot be otherwise. Individual bishops, priests, dioceses, or parishes do not decide on how they will celebrate the liturgy. Liturgy is the unifying and united prayer of the Church.

In his encyclical letter *Ecclesia de Eucharistia*, Pope John Paul II cautioned us,

> I consider it my duty, therefore, to appeal urgently that the liturgical norms for the celebration of the Eucharist be observed with great fidelity. These norms are a concrete expression of the authentically ecclesial nature of the Eucharist; this is their deepest meaning. Liturgy is never anyone's private property, be it of the celebrant or of the community in which the mysteries are celebrated.[6]

Because liturgical changes are given, reception can sometimes be a challenge, especially if adequate prior consultation has not happened. So it becomes even more important that priests understand the changes so as to faithfully integrate the changes into their celebration of the Eucharist.

---

6    Pope John Paul II, Encyclical *Ecclesia de Eucharistia* (EDE) (Washington, DC: USCCB, 2003), no. 52.

Pope Benedict XVI, in *Sacramentum caritatis*, reminds priests of their responsibility to embrace the liturgy the Church provides us:

Emphasizing the importance of the *ars celebrandi* also leads to an appreciation of the value of the liturgical norms. The *ars celebrandi* should foster a sense of the sacred and the use of outward signs which help to cultivate this sense. . . . The eucharistic celebration is enhanced when priests and liturgical leaders are committed to making known the current liturgical texts and norms.[7]

Thorough reflection, dialogue, and discussion by all involved can ease reception and foster a greater and more willing embrace of the changes.

It would be helpful to keep Bridges's stages of transition in mind as we walk people through the process of receiving the new *Roman Missal*. The new *Roman Missal* will disrupt some of what priests and people have been taught to do and say since Vatican II. They will need to know why. Why has the Church established new criteria for translation? Why has the Church modified people's responses at Mass? How will these changes enhance our celebration of the Eucharist?

# CORE CONCERNS

Let us consider what changes we most need to focus on at this time. Changes that will happen as a result of the implementation of the new *Roman Missal* are not momentous but are nevertheless significant.

Introducing a process to help people to understand the changes that will take place with the new translation can be an opportunity also to address two core concerns for the Church: namely, bringing people back to the household of faith and reviving people's sense of liturgy, which "stands at the center of the church's life."[8]

We know that many have left the Church. They no longer partake in the eucharistic celebration. They have drifted off to other

---

7   SacCar, no. 40.

8   EDE, no. 3.

churches or are simply not attending any church. The liturgy for them is in no way "the source and summit of the Christian life."[9]

Even among practicing Catholics, many do not understand well the centrality of the Eucharist in their lives as disciples of Christ. There is a need for much more catechesis. The initiative to help people understand the changes in the *Roman Missal* needs to be broadened to include extensive catechesis on what it means to be a Church of the Eucharist.

We should take advantage of this moment by addressing not only the changes that will take place but also these core concerns for the Church today. We need to address the heart of the matter. Today, far too many could not care less about liturgy—or faith, for that matter—and many know little about the meaning of liturgy.

We are still far from communities who live out "full, conscious, and active participation" in the liturgical assembly, as described by the Second Vatican Council.[10] Many are present, yet unengaged—present, but distracted—present, but passive. They sing little. They pray little. The words and gestures do not find a home in their hearts. After so many years of effort, we are far from realizing the goal that Vatican II envisioned. That cries out for our attention.

# EXPANSIVE CATECHESIS ON THE MEANING OF LITURGY

Now is the time to develop a comprehensive plan to launch an expansive catechesis about liturgy that will prepare our communities for the upcoming changes.

Many foundational documents are available to support this catechesis and to enhance people's broader understanding of the liturgy: *Sacrosanctum Concilium*, from Vatican II (December 4, 1963); the encyclical letters *Mirae caritatis* of Leo XIII (May 28, 1902), *Mediator Dei* of Pius XII (November 20, 1947), *Mysterium fidei* of Paul VI (September 3, 1965), and *Ecclesia de Eucharistia* of John Paul II (April 17, 2003); the apostolic letter *Dies Domini* by John Paul II (May 31, 1998); and the post-synodal apostolic exhortation *Sacramentum caritatis* of Pope Benedict XVI.

---

9    Second Vatican Council, *Lumen gentium*, no. 11, in *Vatican Council II: Volume 1: The Conciliar and Post Conciliar Documents*, ed. Austin Flannery (Northport, NY: Costello Publishing, 1996). Hereafter, Vatican II documents cited in this essay come from this edition.

10   Second Vatican Council, *Sacrosanctum Concilium*, no. 14.

Other documents for catechesis might include the *General Instruction of the Roman Missal* (GIRM), as well as some of the liturgical documents and statements of the United States Conference of Catholic Bishops. Most of these documents are not well known. Catechesis will give people a much-needed background in understanding liturgy and will put the changes in a larger context.

Over the last several years in the Diocese of Tucson, I have had opportunities with our priests and people to study and discuss significant papal documents, such as Pope Benedict XVI's *Deus caritas est* and *Spe salvi*. Both Pope John Paul II and Pope Benedict XVI have provided some marvelous texts. People have appreciated the opportunity to delve into these texts. I have been encouraged and surprised at how well these opportunities have been received. The use of technology, such as PowerPoint presentations and digital images, has enhanced the results. These occasions have given people a deeper understanding of the Church's teachings and a desire to know more. This type of engagement around core documents dealing with liturgy could reap rich benefits for our people. Now is the time.

I have heard often how Msgr. Reynold Hillenbrand, when he was the rector of the University of Saint Mary of the Lake in the Archdiocese of Chicago (1936-1944), would make a point of teaching the seminarians about the social encyclicals of the popes to give them a solid immersion in the social teaching of the Church grounded in doctrine and liturgy. Partly as a result of his efforts to teach the encyclicals, a whole cadre of Chicago priests was ordained with a deep sense of social justice. They brought the message of the encyclicals to the people they served. Much good resulted. Many pastoral initiatives began.

One way to prepare our priests and people for the changes to come in liturgy could be an invitation for them to study and to engage in dialogue about the fundamental documents that spell out how the Church draws her life from the Eucharist. Study guides to help people navigate through the documents would help them grow in their understanding of the liturgy.

Another helpful form of catechesis would be to take people through the actions and texts of the liturgy and explain what lies behind these actions and words. Many people lack even a basic understanding of what happens in the liturgy and appreciate the opportunity to learn more.

In order to reach the greatest possible audience, some of the catechesis could take place during the Sunday homily. One liturgical year could be spent developing people's understanding of the liturgy by focusing on core documents.

At the 2009 Synod in Rome on the Word of God in the Life and Mission of the Church, much discussion took place about the homily: its importance and potential. The Synod Fathers reflected on how the homily needs to be more scripturally based, more dynamic, more engaging, and more catechetical. At Sunday Mass, we meet more of our people than in any other setting. As we introduce the changes in the *Roman Missal*, the homily will be critical in enhancing people's understanding of our worship life.

# OBSTACLES TO EXPANSIVE CATECHESIS

Despite our best intentions, efforts to catechize often fall short. It is hard within dioceses and presbyterates to get everyone on board and participating in any project.

We have made several attempts in the Diocese of Tucson to join together to teach people about liturgy. Some parishes participated, but others did not. I know this result is common in other dioceses as well. This experience is frustrating, because the effort falls short if it is made in only some places and not others. Our efforts falter because we are not pulling together, pulling in the same direction. A deep sense of *communio* within dioceses and presbyterates is missing. This keeps us from realizing our pastoral and formational goals. Too often, our dioceses and parishes are households divided.

The initiative to catechize our people about the changes—and, even more so, about the meaning of liturgy—will take a coordinated effort.

# BRINGING PEOPLE BACK TO THE LORD'S TABLE

To address the significant concern about the drift of people from the table of the Lord, dioceses could develop opportunities for people to return home. In radio spots, for example, people who have returned to the Church could witness to what their return has meant to them and invite others to come home.

Parishes could conduct programs inviting Catholics to return. Many such programs are available to assist parishes in taking forthright steps to make people welcome and to help them deal with their anger and alienation. They need to know they are missed and that they have a place at the Lord's table.

This effort, too, would benefit from the full cooperation of the parishes, priests, and parish staffs of the diocese. Re-evangelization of our people remains one of the most pressing tasks for the Church today. When people are not at church, they cannot worship and share in the riches of the eucharistic banquet. We need them to come home.

While launching an intensive catechetical and evangelizing initiative would not directly deal only with the impending changes in the new *Roman Missal*, these efforts are critical to address core issues of drifting away and ignorance about liturgical matters that our Church faces and so desperately needs to address. The issuance of the new *Roman Missal* provides an occasion to intensify our efforts to form people with a fuller understanding of the Eucharist as a mystery to be believed, to be celebrated, and to be lived.

As we consider a process to introduce the changes, I suggest that the process move beyond the minor adaptations that are contemplated in order to engage as well with the major challenges we face.

# LEADERSHIP MATTERS MOST

In developing a process to successfully implement the new English translation of the *Missale Romanum*, we need to remember that leadership bears the responsibility to help the community to understand and adapt to the changes.

Gerard Egan, in his writings about leadership and change,[11] distinguishes between headship and leadership. Headship is about position, but leadership is about results. The essence of leadership is the achievement of results beyond the ordinary.

Leadership in helping priests and people embrace the changes in the *Roman Missal* calls for individuals and groups who understand the challenges and can draw together collaborators to help

---

11    See Gerard Egan, *Change Agent Skills A: Designing and Assessing Excellence* (San Diego, CA: University Associates, 1988); *Change Agent Skills B: Managing Innovation and Change* (San Diego, CA: University Associates, 1988); *Change Agent Skills in Helping and Human Service Settings* (Monterey, CA: Brooks/Cole Publishing Company, 1985).

the community to understand, to accept, and to value the changes that are occurring.

This process will demand creative and innovative ideas for introducing the changes as well as formulating convincing materials that help people on the local level to understand and that present what underlies the changes. Leaders of liturgical change create a climate of collaboration with priests and people on the local level, encouraging them to become creative and innovative in introducing the new *Roman Missal*. Leaders get people to buy in. They are persistent. They never give up even in the face of resistance. They are committed to seeing this project, the implementation of the new *Roman Missal*, through to completion.

Leaders include the bishops' conference, the local bishop, parish priests, deacons, the diocesan liturgical commissions and diocesan worship office, and parish liturgical committees. Leaders also include composers and publishers.

Leaders bear the responsibility of helping people to understand the reasons and aims and to find ways to respond positively to what is changing. Leaders should anticipate the changes that are coming in order to give the community sufficient time to embrace those changes and to help offset any confusion or discord.

Leaders need to be involved early in learning why the changes in liturgy are happening, how to embrace those changes, and what the changes are meant to accomplish.

## UNITED STATES CONFERENCE OF CATHOLIC BISHOPS

The USCCB has already taken the lead by identifying the goal of preparing communities for the changes in the *Roman Missal* as part of its five top priorities for the 2008-2011 time period. In making faith formation and sacramental practice a priority, the Conference has recognized how important it is to develop processes that will assist dioceses in implementing these changes in a positive way. The Conference's insights and action strategies will be very helpful in formulating materials that diocesan leaders can use in developing their own processes for introducing the changes.

At the USCCB level, it would be desirable to produce materials that could be distributed within dioceses and parishes to assist local ministers in introducing the changes. These materials should put the changes into a larger context that would allow people to understand liturgy in a deeper and fuller way.

In 2006 an initiative was undertaken on the invitation of Bishop Arthur Roche, bishop of Leeds and chair of ICEL, to develop materials, including DVDs, to prepare people for the introduction of the new *Roman Missal.* An initial consultation in November 2006 included representatives from the bishops' conferences of England and Wales, the United States, and Australia. Informally known as the Leeds Group, they intended to develop major papers, ministry guides, and bulletin inserts that would help in the formation of the people.

This effort was supported by the USCCB Committee on Divine Worship (then the Committee on the Liturgy) in the hope that materials would be ready for review as soon as possible. Unfortunately, there was difficulty funding the initiative, and it will not realize its goals internationally. Yet cooperative efforts like this can reap great benefits.

The USCCB can and should take the lead at this point to develop materials that can be distributed to assist dioceses and parishes in their effort both to introduce the changes and to further catechize the faithful in divine worship. Taking the form developed by the Leeds Group, these materials could include study papers (like those in this book), DVDs, bulletin announcements, and homily guides. Local communities need this kind of assistance to augment their own local efforts.

## THE LOCAL BISHOP

The local bishop plays a critical role in this process. He needs to be personally involved. He needs to be supportive of the effort, to see its importance. He needs to advocate on behalf of the plan to inform and educate the community. He needs to seize the moment to catechize. He needs to see this as a priority for himself and for the diocese. He needs to offer input and direction for those who will be delegated to carry out this process. He also needs to understand the process of human change and encourage his priests and people to take the space and time for letting go of what has been and for embracing the changes, as Bridges describes. Listening is critical in the change process, as is catechesis of content.

The bishop needs to encourage the priests of the diocese to recognize the importance of their role in the formulation and implementation of a plan that will introduce the changes to the people. They are the ones who must take the lead in catechizing the laity about the liturgy and the changes. The bishop should encourage his priests to draw upon the resources of the bishops' conference, the diocesan office of divine worship, and their own parishioners.

While the local bishop cannot do everything, I have become more and more aware of how critical his role is. The bishop's presence, his involvement, and his encouragement give importance to any initiative. I have experienced that importance in our diocesan effort to involve priests ordained for less than five years to participate in a diocesan continuing education program. At first the program was resisted. I attended every session and insisted that this be given priority among the recently ordained. In time, they began to see its importance. Some of their pastors even complained that the recently ordained were getting so much of the bishop's time. They wondered why they were not getting so much attention. Presence, involvement, and encouragement by the bishop make a difference.

Similarly, the bishop can make clear that the priests' participation is expected. Every organization makes demands on key leaders. They are expected to come to certain important events.

I experienced that at the seminary at the University of Saint Mary of the Lake when I was rector. Some faculty would not come to significant seminary events. In response, we implemented a policy that identified events at three levels. Level-one events required attendance. Level-two events were important, and faculty presence would be likely. Level-three events were left to the discretion of the faculty member to decide whether he or she would attend.

Bishops can enhance the possibility of priests' learning and growing if clearer expectations are communicated. The priests' leadership will affect how the liturgical changes introduced by the translation of the *Roman Missal* will be accepted and effectively implemented. So priests need to be on board, and bishops need to say loudly and clearly, "All aboard!"

## PRIESTS AND PASTORS

Priests, especially pastors, will play a key role—for better or for worse—in this process. If they are cynical, negative, or indifferent, that attitude will deter any effort to deepen the people's understanding of the liturgy and the coming changes. When priests are seen by their people as being eager to learn and desirous to accept and embrace change as the will of the Church, then the people will be inclined to respond in a similar way.

When priests themselves clearly understand the changes and the reasons, as well as the process and practice of leading change, they can more effectively lead the people in understanding and accepting the changes. They will need to be creative and draw upon the resources made available to them by the bishops' conference, diocesan liturgical commissions, offices of worship, and parish liturgy committees.

In every presbyterate, there are priests who are out in front. They prepare for and welcome change. They see the value and importance of the change. They will engage in the process for introducing the liturgical change enthusiastically. They will faithfully implement what is suggested and do so with a positive spirit. Their efforts need to be affirmed by the bishop and held up as an example. Regretfully, too often, more attention is given to those who resist than to those who take the lead.

In every presbyterate there are also those who will go along to get along. They will do what is expected, follow the plan. They will get the job done but will not exercise much leadership. They need to be affirmatively challenged and respectfully reminded of the critical role they play as shepherds of their community.

Finally, in every presbyterate there are those—sometimes the most generous and pastoral priests—who will resist for whatever reason. Some of those priests who resist do not care to put in the time to catechize. They feel burnt out. Some oppose what is happening because they feel cut off from the process or feel the changes are not helpful. Some may just like to be difficult.

It may not be possible to change the latter group, but their opposition needs to be addressed. Because it is not easy, that fraternal correction is not always given. Yet the priests in this group need to hear it. More direct feedback from and even confrontation by the bishop will be needed—given not as scolding but with understanding and respect.

## DEACONS

Deacons assist at many liturgical celebrations. They preach and catechize. They can share the responsibility of holding sessions for parish leaders and parishioners on the why and what of the changes that are happening. Their cooperation and enthusiastic support of this effort on behalf of the parish can add a lot to the effort to catechize. They will need time to learn about the changes and discuss their attitudes and feelings. Special sessions for training and teaching deacons should be a part of every diocesan plan.

## DIOCESAN OFFICES OF DIVINE WORSHIP AND DIOCESAN LITURGICAL COMMISSIONS

Diocesan offices of divine worship and diocesan liturgical commissions can provide parishes with needed expertise in formulating the reasons behind the changes. They can provide the text resources (including study guides) and staff assistance necessary for workshops and seminars. They can help the diocese focus on the core concerns of the Church rather than just on the changes that are coming. They, too, need to understand and manage the change process and not just the content of the changes.

## PARISH LITURGICAL COMMITTEES

Lay ecclesial ministers who are responsible for liturgy in some parishes are where "the rubber meets the road." Along with the pastor, lay ecclesial ministers will need to deliver the message to the people in the pews. They will need to respond to the people's confusion or frustration or resistance—not an easy task. But careful planning and implementation of the diocesan or parish plan to manage the changes will make a difference and result in greater acceptance and smoother transition.

## COMPOSERS AND PUBLISHERS

Composers and publishers will also play a leadership role in the changes that will take place. Composers will need to be prepared and to work diligently during the *vacatio legis* to formulate fitting musical environments for the changed texts. Publishers will need to provide the liturgical books that contain the new translations in attractive layouts that make the texts easy to read and proclaim.

# PROCESS AND TIMELINE

Finally, I suggest a process and timeline for what might be done to guide our people through the changes that will come when the English translation of the *Missale Romanum* of 2002 is finally introduced.

Several types of changes are expected in this third edition of the *Roman Missal*. There will be changes in some of the people's responses. There will be changes in the words of the texts proclaimed in the readings and in the prayers. There will be new texts for the expanded sanctoral cycle, for new votive Masses, and for new Masses for special occasions. There may even be some new changes to be introduced, like the movement of the sign of peace.

Again, I believe strongly that the two core concerns facing the Church today—catechizing people on the liturgy and inviting people to come back to the Lord's table—need to be linked to the process of introducing the changes. I believe that if those are not addressed, our efforts to introduce the changes will have little lasting result.

Here I suggest three stages for the process to manage the upcoming change. The first covers the present time before *recognitio* by the Holy See; the second covers the period after *recognitio* and before implementation; and the third covers the period during and after implementation. These stages correspond to Bridges's three phases of transition.

 ## STAGE ONE: REMOTE PREPARATION

This is a time for intensive catechesis on the liturgy. If catechesis is embraced by the entire Church in the United States and within dioceses, we will see positive results in people's understanding and awareness of the liturgy.

If we focus our efforts, staying fixed on this objective of liturgical catechesis without being diverted, communities will be ready for the introduction of the new *Roman Missal*. But staying focused will not be easy.

I have seen in my own diocese how hard it is to stay focused on a particular objective. We begin but do not stay the course. We get drawn into pressing issues and cease giving priority to what is important. Leaders—the bishop and pastoral leaders—need to keep their eyes fixed on the goal, like the archer intent in his focus on the target.

The first step in this stage is the **development of catechetical materials** that could be used by parishes. This is the responsibility of the bishops' conference, with the help of offices of worship and liturgical scholars and consultants. The materials should be diverse, creative, and comprehensive. They should include resources for the leadership of dioceses and parishes and materials for distribution in parishes. Technology can expand the availability of the materials and enrich their presentation.

The materials might guide people through core liturgical documents, beginning with *Sacrosanctum Concilium* and progressing to significant Vatican and bishops' statements on liturgy.

The second step is **distribution and use of the materials** for instruction and formation of the faithful in the worship life of the Church. This should be done in as expansive and creative a way as possible. Video streaming, DVDs, and video conferencing can enhance the opportunities for instruction. Diocesan and parish Web sites can walk people through the documents. Parishes can invite parishioners to sign up to receive e-mails with quotes or teachings from core liturgical documents.

A series of homilies, preferably given throughout the year, can touch upon the history of liturgy, the *Roman Missal*, the structure of the Mass, the way in which liturgy deepens our spiritual lives and our encounter with Christ, the importance of symbol and gesture, and other pertinent reflections.

Dioceses and parishes may want to conduct liturgical workshops for groups that are already meeting regularly, like diocesan or parish pastoral councils, school boards, and groups of parents whose children are receiving sacraments. Parish groups such as catechists, Catholic school teachers, extraordinary ministers of Holy Communion, and lectors could be invited to receive some instruction on the liturgy whenever they gather or convene. As much as possible, this instruction can be integrated into what the diocese or parish is already doing.

Schools and religious education programs might focus on liturgy by finding ways to integrate teaching on liturgy into their syllabi in age-appropriate ways.

"Catechize, catechize, catechize" would be the refrain of this period.

The third step would be the **introduction and integration of mystagogy** into the formation in liturgy begun in step two. A mystagogical process invites us to encounter and experience the person of Christ, not just to learn information or to study the sacred mysteries and the teachings of the Church. Our people need to experience beautifully celebrated liturgy that leads them to an encounter with Christ.

When we celebrate Mass, we participate in the holy and divine liturgy—the great mystery. The Synod on the Word occasioned many reflections about the Emmaus journeyers who encountered Christ on the road. That encounter turned their lives around. It was only after their encounter that the words of Scripture became alive in their hearts. So our instruction in step three cannot be given in words alone; it needs to be a transforming experience grounded in prayer.

As Pope Benedict XVI said in *Sacramentum caritatis*, "A mystagogical catechesis must also be concerned with *presenting the meaning of the signs* contained in the rites. . . . More than simply conveying information; a mystagogical catechesis should be capable of making the faithful more sensitive to the language of signs and gestures which, together with the word, make up the rite."[12]

Some have voiced concern that, since Vatican II, we have lost a sense of mystery in the celebration of the Eucharist. Reverence has given way to familiarity. Liturgy has become too wordy, lacking in the experience of the Divine.

Again in *Sacramentum caritatis*, Pope Benedict reflects, "A convincing indication of the effectiveness of eucharistic catechesis is surely an increased sense of the mystery of God present among us. . . . I am thinking in general of the importance of gestures and posture."[13]

This period of catechesis prior to *recognitio* would be an opportunity to strive to make our liturgical celebrations occasions to encounter the Living Christ. This encounter is made more possible through use of silence, reverence in the use of symbols and gestures, deliberateness in the celebration—all of which teaches that this action in which we are engaged is indeed a mystery beyond our grasp, an encounter with the Living God.

This third step of stage one could become an expansive diocesan and parish effort to call back home those who have left the Church. Too many have walked away, for a wide range of reasons. The introduction of the third edition of the *Roman Missal* could be the occasion for reminding us of the empty seats at the table and our longing to bring family members back home.

---

12  SacCar, no. 64.

13  SacCar, no. 65.

This will take effort and outreach. Yet people respond when they trust someone is interested in their well-being.

Such an evangelization initiative would be a welcome partner alongside the effort to form people more deeply in their understanding and celebrating of the Eucharist.

"Invite, invite, invite!" would be the year's refrain as well.

Clearly, this time prior to the *recognitio* of the Holy See would be a busy, challenging time as well as an innovative and creative time. If we are going to lead people to understand and receive the changes that are coming, it would be best to do this in the context of a broad and expansive liturgical formation as well as a widespread evangelizing initiative. Catechize and invite.

## 2 STAGE TWO: VACATIO LEGIS: TIME BETWEEN RECOGNITIO AND IMPLEMENTATION

Stage two begins with the *recognitio* and continues through the time when the changes are implemented. This may not be an extended period of time, but it is a crucial time to outline the changes and prepare priests and deacons, liturgical ministers, and the worshiping community for what is to come.

Step one of stage two is a **focused effort to prepare priests, deacons, lectors, musicians, and all involved in the liturgical celebration** for the changes.

Priests and deacons especially will need to gather to become familiar with the revised texts, practice proclaiming them, and in general renew their acquaintance with the Sacramentary and Lectionary. This will be an opportunity to remind the priest of his critical role as presider at the liturgy and as the one who acts *in persona Christi*.

Pope Benedict says, in *Sacramentum caritatis*,

> Priests should be conscious of the fact that in their ministry they must never put themselves or their personal opinions in first place, but Jesus Christ. . . . The priest is above all a servant of others, and he must continually work at being a sign pointing to Christ, a docile instrument in the Lord's hands. This is seen particularly in his humility in leading the liturgical assembly, in obedience to the rite, uniting himself to it in mind and heart, and avoiding anything that

might give the impression of an inordinate emphasis on his own personality.[14]

When the bishop gathers his priests, this gathering can be not only an occasion for fraternity but also an opportunity to be reminded of the awesome responsibility the priest has in presiding at the Eucharist and the leadership role he plays as shepherd of his parish.

At these gatherings, the bishop can emphasize that priests need to understand better the challenges of translating sacred texts. It will be important for priests to understand *Liturgiam authenticam* as the guiding document from the Vatican used in developing the most recent translations.

This can be an opportunity for extensive dialogue between a bishop and his priests, with time allotted for raising their questions or for expressing their concerns. Priests need to be listened to and supported. They need to understand that even if they do not fully agree with the changes, they preside at the Eucharist *in persona Christi*, not in their own name.

Priests will have the primary responsibility of introducing the changes to their people. If priests are cynical or negative, the changes will be poorly received, even met with resistance. So the priests need to discuss their feelings and get their frustrations out if they are to be open to what the Church is saying and teaching.

Musicians and composers, too, will need to become familiar with the revised texts when they are set to new arrangements. Even more importantly, they need to be reminded of the importance of music as sung prayer. They do not merely perform music; they lead people in giving praise to God in song.

The new *Roman Missal* will provide a new opportunity to teach priests, deacons, and people the dialogic chants of the liturgy, so that they can really sing the liturgy, not just sing at liturgy. When we sing texts, we can more readily remember them and can more easily reflect upon them.

The second step of stage two involves **acquainting the people with the changes that will happen**, especially in the people's responses. They, too, need to understand why the changes in wording are taking place. This could be communicated in diocesan newspapers, in a series of bulletin articles, or in a series of brief, concise comments after the final prayer, made from the pulpit,

---

over the course of several weeks. There should be opportunities for parishioners to practice the responses and become more comfortable with changes to prayers they have come to know by heart.

# 3 STAGE THREE: DURING AND AFTER IMPLEMENTATION

Stage three begins with the implementation of the changes in the celebration of the Eucharist. Whether this goes well depends on the extent to which stages one and two have been implemented. The transition will be very smooth when the celebrant, liturgical ministers, and the community understand what to expect and why things have changed.

If a parish's only plan is to introduce the changes on the very first Sunday they are to be used, the results will most likely be confusion and liturgical disaster. Preparation for change is important; if that is left out, what occurs will be a mess. People will make different responses, wonder why the changes are there, feel confused, and leave the celebration feeling frustrated or angry.

A very different result will occur when proper and extensive catechesis has taken place and when the changes are introduced reverently and respectfully. Such implementation will allow people to realize that the changes do not distract or deter from the liturgy but add value to its celebration.

Over time these minor changes will be well integrated into the celebration of the Eucharist, and priests and people will adjust. It will become even clearer that the effort to catechize people on liturgy and invite them to come home to the Church will reap the greatest benefit of all of the work undertaken in preparation for the new *Roman Missal*.

# CONCLUSION

The changes in the translation of the new *Roman Missal* will occur. That is a given. But what is not given is how we will prepare priests, deacons, and people for those changes. That preparation is critical for how the changes will be received.

The process will be messy, disruptive, and divisive unless our priests, deacons, and people are prepared for the changes. This preparation involves giving them time to grieve what is changing, presenting them with the "what" and "why" of the changes, and walking with them through the adjustments that need to be made.

My invitation is to prepare far more broadly than just for the changes that will come into effect. See this moment as a grand opportunity.

Make this an opportunity for re-instruction about the whole liturgical tradition of the Church, which is little known or understood by the faithful. Look at what is new and what is old, and show the continuity that exists even as worship has changed.

Make this an opportunity to enrich the proclamation of the Word as it is read, to improve the content and delivery of homilies, to enhance the aesthetic movement of the liturgy, to deepen the sense of the sacred, and to add to the beauty of our churches and the care given to them.

The celebration of the Eucharist, regardless of the translation of the texts, becomes diminished through bad homilies, poor musical leadership and participation, unintelligible reading, or sloppy or careless preparation for the celebration of the divine liturgy.

Make this an opportunity to enliven people's desire to return home and to welcome them on their return.

Make this occasion a needed chance to catechize, evangelize, and sing to the Lord a new song. That will reap many benefits.

Liturgy is the source and summit of our life in Christ. We ought not to miss this opportunity to reintroduce our priests and people to the beauty and mystery of the eucharistic celebration.

The changes can be an occasion for a reawakening of the liturgical life of the Church, a new beginning.

# CHAPTER 2

# Liturgical Implementation of the *Roman Missal*

REV. JOHN J. M. FOSTER, JCD

The Second Vatican Council's *Constitution on the Liturgy, Sacrosanctum Concilium*, reiterates that the liturgy forms part of the treasury of the Church.[1] For this reason, no one can be permitted "to feel free to treat it lightly and with disregard for its sacredness and its universality."[2] Liturgical law, then, provides order to the celebration of the Church's liturgy, including the celebration of the Eucharist. Such order seeks to ensure not only that liturgical celebrations are of good quality but also that the liturgy celebrated expresses the faith of the Church and that the common good of the Christian faithful is maintained, protecting their right to authentic celebrations.[3]

As those entrusted to shepherd the flock of Christ, the bishops have the first responsibility to regulate the liturgy. Nevertheless, this responsibility is not theirs alone. In exercising their sanctifying function in the particular church entrusted to them, the bishops

---

1    See Second Vatican Council, *Sacrosanctum Concilium* (SC), no. 26, December 4, 1963, AAS 56 (1964) 107. See also Pope John Paul II, Encyclical letter *Ecclesia de Eucharistia* (EDE), no. 52, AAS 95 (2003) 468: "Liturgy is never anyone's private property, be it of the celebrant or of the community in which the mysteries are celebrated." English translation from *Ecclesia de Eucharistia* (Washington, DC: United States Conference of Catholic Bishops [USCCB]); hereafter translations of this document will be taken from this source.

2    EDE, no. 52.

3    See *Codex Iuris Canonici auctoritate Ioannis Pauli PP. II promulgatus* (Vatican City: Libreria Editrice Vaticana, 1983), c. 214: "The Christian faithful have the right to worship God according to the prescripts of their own rite approved by the legitimate pastors of the Church and to follow their own form of spiritual life so long as it is consonant with the doctrine of the Church." English translation from *Code of Canon Law, Latin-English Edition: New English Translation* (2nd ed.) (Washington, DC: Canon Law Society of America, 2001). Hereafter, unless otherwise indicated, all citations from the *Code of Canon Law* refer to the 1983 *Code*.

are assisted by their presbyters, ministers, and other lay faithful. This paper will examine the liturgical and canonical responsibilities entrusted to diocesan bishops and their various collaborators at the diocesan and parish levels in implementing the forthcoming English translation of the third typical edition of the *Missale Romanum*.[4] This examination, however, will be all the more profitable when situated in its proper context. For this reason, we will begin with a review of those ecclesiastical authorities competent to regulate the Church's liturgy.

# THE AUTHORITIES COMPETENT TO REGULATE THE LITURGY

Repeating *Sacrosanctum Concilium*, paragraph 22, almost verbatim, canon 838 §1 of the 1983 *Code of Canon Law* states: "The direction [*moderatio*] of the sacred liturgy depends solely on the authority of the Church which resides in the Apostolic See and, according to the norm of law, the diocesan bishop." The next three paragraphs of the canon specify the general functions for the Apostolic See, the conference of bishops, and the diocesan bishop in the regulation of the liturgy.

## THE APOSTOLIC SEE

From the Council of Trent to the Second Vatican Council, essentially one authority was competent to regulate the liturgy: the Apostolic See.[5] Indeed, canon 1257 of the 1917 *Code of Canon Law* stated: "It belongs only to the Apostolic See to order sacred liturgy and to approve liturgical books."[6] Pope Pius XII repeated this discipline

---

4 *Missale Romanum, ex decreto Sacrosancti Oecumenici Concilii Vaticani II instauratum autoritate Pauli PP. VI promulgatum Ioannis Pauli PP. II cura recognitum, editio typica tertia* (Vatican City: Typis Vaticanis, 2002). Hereafter, the 2002 *Missale Romanum* will be cited as *Missale Romanum, editio typica tertia.*

5 In accord with 1983 *Code of Canon Law*, c. 361, the term "Apostolic See" includes not only the Roman Pontiff but also the Secretariat of State and other institutes in the Roman Curia.

6 *Codex Iuris Canonici Pii X Pontificis Maximi iussu digestus Benedicti Papae XV auctoritate promulgatus* (Rome: Typis Polyglottis Vaticanis, 1917). English translation taken from Edward N. Peters, ed., *The 1917 Pio-Benedictine Code of Canon Law in English Translation* (San Francisco: Ignatius Press, 2001); hereafter, all citations specifically from the 1917 *Code* come from this source.

in his 1947 encyclical *Mediator Dei*.[7] Only with the promulgation of *Sacrosanctum Concilium* in 1963 did the strict centralization concerning the regulation of the liturgy ease. Even though conferences of bishops and diocesan bishops were recognized as having authority to regulate the liturgy in accord with the norm of law, the Apostolic See continues to play an essential role.

The general competence of the Apostolic See vis-à-vis the regulation of the liturgy is found in canon 838 §2 of the 1983 *Code of Canon Law*: "It is for the Apostolic See to order the sacred liturgy of the universal Church, publish liturgical books and review their translations in vernacular languages, and exercise vigilance that liturgical regulations are observed faithfully everywhere." Pope John Paul II further specified the Apostolic See's liturgical authority when he detailed the competence of the Congregation for the Divine Worship and the Discipline of the Sacraments in the 1988 apostolic constitution *Pastor bonus* (nos. 62-70).[8]

## CONFERENCES OF BISHOPS

While conferences of bishops have existed since the nineteenth century, they were granted juridic authority only at the Second Vatican Council.[9] In conferences of bishops, the bishops of a nation or territory "jointly exercise certain pastoral functions for the Christian faithful of their territory in order to promote the greater good which the Church offers to humanity, especially through forms and programs of the apostolate fittingly adapted to the circumstances of time and place, according to the norm of law" (c. 447). Inasmuch as the liturgy is an important pastoral function, the conference of bishops exercises its authority in accord with the norm of law for the Christian faithful in its territory. In practical terms, this means that liturgical books and norms lawfully approved by one conference of bishops cannot be used in another conference.[10]

*Sacrosanctum Concilium* recognized that conferences of bishops can play an important role in regulating the liturgy for their respective

---

7   See Pius XII, Encyclical letter *Mediator Dei*, November 20, 1947, AAS 39 (1947) 544.

8   See John Paul II, Apostolic constitution *Pastor bonus*, June 28, 1988, AAS 80 (1988) 876-878.

9   See SC, no. 22; see also Second Vatican Council, Decree *Christus Dominus*, nos. 36-38, October 28, 1965, AAS 58 (1966) 692-694.

10  See Congregation for Divine Worship and the Discipline of the Sacraments, Instruction *Liturgiam authenticam*, nos. 83-84, March 28, 2001, AAS 93 (2001) 713.

territories. Specifically, this includes the decision to permit the use of vernacular languages in liturgical celebrations and the adaptation—whether foreseen or not—of the liturgical books issued by the Apostolic See.[11] Canon 838 §3 of the 1983 *Code* established the liturgical competence of the conference of bishops in this way: "It pertains to the conferences of bishops to prepare and publish, after the prior review of the Holy See, translations of liturgical books in vernacular languages, adapted appropriately within the limits defined in the liturgical books themselves." Although conferences of bishops must observe the norms of the 2001 instruction *Liturgiam authenticam* for the translation of liturgical books, most of the liturgical books issued since the Second Vatican Council include a section near the end of the *praenotanda* listing possible adaptations that conferences of bishops might choose to make. Such a list for the celebration of the Eucharist is contained in Chapter IX of the *Institutio Generalis Missalis Romani*.[12] On November 14, 2001, the United States Conference of Catholic Bishops (USCCB) approved "Adaptations of the *Institutio Generalis Missalis Romani, editio typica tertia*, for the Dioceses of the United States of America." The adaptations were granted *recognitio* by the Congregation for the Divine Worship and the Discipline of the Sacraments on April 17, 2002, and were promulgated on April 25, 2002, by the Most Reverend Wilton Gregory, then president of the USCCB, for immediate implementation.[13]

## THE DIOCESAN BISHOP

If, as noted above, the Apostolic See alone regulated the liturgy prior to the Second Vatican Council, what was the task of the bishop during that period? Canon 1261 §1 of the 1917 *Code* stated: "Local Ordinaries shall be vigilant that the prescriptions of the sacred can-

---

11    See SC, nos. 36, 38-40, and 63.

12    *Institutio Generalis Missalis Romani* (IGMR), nos. 386-399, in *Missale Romanum, editio typica tertia*; hereafter, unless otherwise indicated, the abbreviation IGMR will refer to the 2002 text. It should be noted that the Latin title and abbreviation of this document will also be used to differentiate it from its English translation, the *General Instruction of the Roman Missal* (GIRM). This differentiation is necessary because of a decision by the Congregation for Divine Worship and the Discipline of the Sacraments to insert conference adaptations at their proper place in the English translation, thus replacing the Latin text of the universal law. See *Liturgiam authenticam*, no. 69. While the English text is a legitimate vernacular translation of the *editio typica*, there are passages in the former that do not appear in the latter, and vice versa.

13    See USCCB Bishops' Committee on the Liturgy, *Newsletter* 38 (May 2002): 69.

ons on divine cult be scrupulously observed, and especially lest there be introduced in divine cult, whether public or private, or in the daily life of the faithful, any superstitious practice or that in any way there be admitted anything alien to the faith or inconsistent with ecclesiastic tradition or anything looking like a sort of profit." In other words, the bishop's responsibility boiled down to ensuring that the Holy See's regulations were observed faithfully.[14]

As noted above, paragraph 22 of *Sacrosanctum Concilium* states that the regulation of the liturgy depends not only on the Apostolic See but also on the diocesan bishop, according to the norm of law. Unlike the authority of the Apostolic See, the liturgical authority of the diocesan bishop is circumscribed by the law. More specifically, canon 838 §4 of the 1983 *Code* states: "Within the limits of his competence, it pertains to the diocesan bishop in the Church entrusted to him to issue liturgical norms which bind everyone." In other words, liturgical norms issued by a diocesan bishop are observed only within the territory of his diocese and apply only to liturgical rites of the Latin Church.[15] Such norms even bind members of religious institutes and societies of apostolic life (see cc. 678 §1 and 738 §1).

# THE IMPLEMENTATION OF THE *ROMAN MISSAL* IN THE DIOCESAN CHURCH

The implementation of the vernacular translation of the third typical edition of the *Missale Romanum* does not fall to the diocesan bishop alone. While he certainly plays an instrumental role in this process, he can and should rely on assistance from his collaborators in diocesan ministry. This section explores the liturgical role of the diocesan bishop as well as those of various groups and officeholders in the particular church. Finally, attention is given to key points in the process of implementation of the *Roman Missal* in the diocese.

---

14    Pius XII reiterated this duty in *Mediator Dei* (AAS 39 [1947] 544).

15    See Frederick R. McManus, "Introductory Canons (cc. 834-839)," in *New Commentary on the Code of Canon Law,* ed. John P. Beal et al. (New York/Mahwah, NJ: Paulist Press, 2000), 1016.

## THE ROLE OF THE DIOCESAN BISHOP

Canon 835 §1 of the *Code of Canon Law* sets forth the sanctifying function of the bishop: "The bishops in the first place exercise the sanctifying function; they are the high priests, the principal dispensers of the mysteries of God, and the directors, promoters, and guardians of the entire liturgical life in the church entrusted to them." Although the norm clearly establishes the bishop's governance function vis-à-vis the liturgy (i.e., director, promoter, and guardian), what is often overlooked is the liturgical role played by the bishop himself: he is a high priest who celebrates the liturgy. In other words, the bishop exercises his sanctifying office through his liturgical presence and example. *Sacrosanctum Concilium*, paragraph 41, states eloquently the bishop's liturgical role:

> The bishop is to be looked upon as the high priest of his flock, the faithful's life in Christ in some way deriving from and depending on him.
>
> Therefore all should hold in great esteem the liturgical life of the diocese centered around the bishop, especially in his cathedral church; they must be convinced that the preeminent manifestation of the Church is present in the full, active participation of all God's holy people in these liturgical celebrations, especially in the same eucharist, in a single prayer, at one altar at which the bishop presides, surrounded by his college of priests and by his ministers.[16]

Indeed, the *Caeremoniale Episcoporum* emphasizes that liturgical celebrations at which the bishop presides "should also serve as a model for the entire diocese and be shining examples of active

---

16    SC, no. 41. English translation in *Documents on the Liturgy, 1963-1979: Conciliar, Papal, and Curial Texts* (DOL), trans. and ed. International Commission on English in the Liturgy (ICEL) (Collegeville, MN: The Liturgical Press, 1982), margin reference 41. Hereafter, texts from the DOL will include citations to the DOL followed by the margin reference.

participation by the people."[17] The *Institutio Generalis Missalis Romani* explicates this norm:

> The Bishop should therefore be determined that the priests, the deacons, and the lay Christian faithful grasp ever more deeply the genuine meaning of the rites and liturgical texts, and thereby be led to an active and fruitful celebration of the Eucharist. To the same end, he should also be vigilant that the dignity of these celebrations be enhanced. In promoting this dignity, the beauty of the sacred place, of music, and of art should contribute as greatly as possible.[18]

As mentioned previously, the bishop exercises the sanctifying office not only through his liturgical presence but also as a director, promoter, and guardian of the liturgical life in his diocese. As the director (*moderator*) of liturgy in the diocese, the bishop can make use of the legislative, executive, and judicial power that is his in virtue of his office of diocesan bishop (see c. 391). Moreover, this power is ordinary, proper, and immediate (see c. 381). With regard to the celebration of the Eucharist, IGMR, paragraph 387, entrusts to the diocesan bishop the regulation of the following: the discipline of concelebration, establishment of norms concerning the function of altar servers, the distribution of Holy Communion under both kinds, and the construction and ordering of churches. As promoter of the liturgy, the bishop encourages the liturgical apostolate in his particular church. He does this not only by his own actions but also through his liturgical collaborators. Whenever the bishop encourages liturgical ministers and provides for the continued liturgical formation and catechesis of the clergy, ministers, and lay faithful, he promotes the liturgy. Finally, as the guardian (*custos*) of the liturgy, the bishop safeguards the integrity of the liturgy as handed on by the Church. He ensures that liturgical norms are observed (including

---

17  *Caeremoniale Episcoporum, ex decreto Sacrosancti Oecumenici Concilii Vaticani II instauratum auctoritate Ioannis Pauli Pp. VI promulgatum, editio typica*, September 14, 1984 (Typis Polyglottis Vaticanis, 1985), 12; English translation from *Ceremonial of Bishops*, trans. ICEL (Collegeville, MN: The Liturgical Press, 1989). See also Pope Benedict XVI, Apostolic exhortation *Sacramentum caritatis* (SacCar), no. 39, February 22, 2007, AAS 99 (2007) 136-137.

18  IGMR, no. 22; English translation taken from *General Instruction of the Roman Missal* (Washington, DC: USCCB, 2003); hereafter all translations will be quoted from this source unless otherwise indicated.

those permitting adaptations and accommodations foreseen in the liturgical books) as well as correcting any abuses that occur.[19]

## COLLABORATORS WITH THE DIOCESAN BISHOP

As noted above, the diocesan bishop can and should rely on the assistance of his closest collaborators in implementing the revised *Roman Missal*. Counted first among the diocesan bishop's collaborators are the priests—whether presbyters or other bishops—working in the diocese. Other collaborators who will play an important role in the implementation process can be found in the diocesan curia, e.g., the diocesan liturgical commission, the office for worship, and vicars general and episcopal.

### Presbyters

The 2004 *Directory for the Pastoral Ministry of Bishops, Apostolorum successores*, observes that

> diocesan priests, in fact, are the principal and irreplaceable co-workers of the order of Bishops, invested with the unique and identical ministerial priesthood which the Bishop possesses in its fullness. The Bishop and the priests are constituted as ministers of the apostolic mission. The priests share in the Bishop's solicitude and responsibility in such a way that together they nurture an ecclesial sense at once local and universal.[20]

Canon 835 §2 makes this same point with regard to the sanctifying office: "Presbyters also exercise this [sanctifying] function; sharing in the priesthood of Christ and as his ministers under the authority of the bishop, they are consecrated to celebrate divine worship and to sanctify the people."

It is the priests of the diocese—whether they serve as pastors, as parochial vicars, as chaplains to various communities, or in some other ministry—who not only will bear the immediate responsibility for implementing the new *Roman Missal* in their respective

---

19   See Congregation for Divine Worship and the Discipline of the Sacraments, Instruction *Redemptionis sacramentum*, nos. 21-24, March 25, 2004, AAS 96 (2004) 556-557.

20   Congregation for Bishops, *Apostolorum successores* (Vatican City: Libreria Editrice Vaticana, 2004), no. 75.

communities but will also largely determine by their own demeanor how well the revised liturgical book is accepted by the Christian faithful in the diocese. As with the bishop's implementation, the way in which the priest celebrates the Eucharist using the revised *Roman Missal* can go far in catechizing the faithful in its meaning and in deepening their participation. The *Directory on the Ministry and Life of Priests* observes:

> In a society ever more sensitive to communication through signs and images, the priest must pay adequate attention to all of that which can enhance the decorum and sacredness of the Eucharistic celebration. . . . In fact, a lack of attention to the symbolic aspects of the liturgy and, even more, carelessness and coldness, superficiality and disorder, empty the meaning and weaken the process of strengthening the faith. Those who improperly celebrate the Mass reveal a weakness in their faith and fail to educate the others in the faith. Celebrating the Eucharist well, however, constitutes a highly important catechesis on the Sacrifice.[21]

Priests should not be afraid to work with the diocesan bishop in implementing the new *Roman Missal*, offering their insights gained from pastoral experience.[22] As priests work together and with the bishop, reflecting on the liturgical norms and new English translation of the prayers and other texts, not only will their own understanding of the eucharistic mystery be deepened, but their unity of purpose, under the direction of the bishop, will be clear to the Christian faithful.

One cannot underestimate the importance of involving all the priests in the diocese in the plan to implement the revised *Roman Missal*. However, in those dioceses where the number of priests is large or where the priests cannot easily gather together, such universal participation might not be possible. In these cases, priests might be convoked by vicariate or deanery to meet with the bishop and the liturgical collaborators mentioned below. Moreover, inasmuch as the presbyteral council, which is a group of priests representing the entire presbyterate, "assists the bishop in the governance of the diocese according to the norm of law to promote as

---

21 Congregation for the Clergy, *Directory on the Ministry and Life of Priests* (Washington, DC: USCCB, 1994), no. 49.

22 See *Directory on the Ministry and Life of Priests*, nos. 24 and 65.

much as possible the pastoral good of the portion of the people of God entrusted to him" (c. 495 §1), the diocesan bishop might find it especially helpful to bring the implementation plan to this consultative group for its review.

One cannot underestimate the importance of having the priests on board with the diocesan plan to implement the third edition of the *Roman Missal*. As human psychology and past experience have taught, the effectiveness of a person's catechesis is proportionate to his or her internal appropriation of the values and discipline at issue.

## Diocesan Curia

At the diocesan level, various institutes—whether groups or offices—"assist the bishop in the governance of the whole diocese, especially in guiding pastoral action" (c. 469). "The Bishop *freely appoints* the heads of the various curial offices from among those who distinguish themselves by competence in their respective fields of expertise, by pastoral zeal and by the integrity of their Christian life, taking care not to entrust offices or tasks to those lacking the necessary skills."[23] Regarding the implementation of the revised *Roman Missal*, three curial institutes deserve attention: the diocesan liturgical commission, the office for worship, and vicars general and episcopal.

### Diocesan Liturgical Commission

While diocesan commissions for music and sacred art emerged during the pontificates of Popes Pius X and Pius XI, the diocesan commission on liturgy was recommended by Pope Pius XII in *Mediator Dei*.[24] At the Second Vatican Council, however, the diocesan liturgical commission became a required institute in the diocesan curia. *Sacrosanctum Concilium* states:

---

23 *Apostolorum successores*, no. 176; emphasis in the original.

24 For a brief history of the development of commissions for liturgy, music, and art during the first half of the twentieth century, see John J. M. Foster, *Liturgical Commissions and Offices: A Resource Book* (Washington, DC: Federation of Diocesan Liturgical Commissions, 2001), 14-20; see also Foster, "Diocesan Commissions for Liturgy, Music, and Art: Endangered Species?", *Worship* 71 (March 1997): 125-129.

Every diocese is to have a commission on the liturgy, under the direction of the bishop, for promoting the liturgical apostolate.

Sometimes it may be advisable for several dioceses to form among themselves one single commission, in order to promote the liturgy by means of shared consultation.

Besides the commission on the liturgy, every diocese, as far as possible, should have commissions for music and art.

These three commissions must work in closest collaboration; indeed it will often be best to fuse the three of them into one single commission.[25]

Nearly eight weeks after the promulgation of *Sacrosanctum Concilium*, Pope Paul VI promulgated the *motu proprio Sacram liturgiam* to implement certain provisions of the liturgy constitution, among which were the articles concerning diocesan commissions for liturgy, music, and art.[26] It was not until the Consilium and Congregation of Rites issued the instruction *Inter oecumenici* on September 26, 1964, that the role and function of liturgical commissions were explicated:

47. The diocesan liturgical commission, under the direction of the bishop, has these responsibilities:

a.  to be fully informed on the state of pastoral-liturgical activity in the diocese;

b.  to carry out faithfully those proposals in liturgical matters made by the competent authority and to keep

---

25  SC, nos. 45-46 (DOL 45-46). For an examination of the development of SC, nos. 45-46, see Foster, *Liturgical Commissions and Offices*, 21-30.

26  See Paul VI, *Motu proprio Sacram liturgiam*, January 25, 1964, AAS 56 (1964) 141:

In keeping with the norms of art. 45 and 46, in all dioceses there is to be a commission that is entrusted, under the bishop's direction, with the duty of increasing the knowledge and furthering the progress of the liturgy.

In this matter it may be advantageous for several dioceses to have a joint commission.

Each diocese should also, as far as possible, have two other commissions, one for music, the other for art.

In some dioceses it will often be advisable to merge the three commissions into one. (DOL 280)

informed on the studies and programs taking place elsewhere in this field;

c.   to suggest and promote practical programs of every kind that may contribute to the advancement of liturgical life, especially in the interest of aiding priests laboring in the Lord's vineyard;

d.   to suggest, in individual cases or even for the whole diocese, timely, step-by-step measures for the work of pastoral liturgy, to appoint and to call upon people capable of helping priests in this matter as occasion arises, to propose suitable means and resources;

e.   to see to it that programs in the diocese designed to promote liturgy go forward with the cooperation and mutual help of other groups along the lines mentioned above ([*Inter oecumenici,*] no. 45e) regarding the liturgical commission of the assembly of bishops.[27]

The diocesan liturgical commission is composed of men and women, clerics and lay faithful, who are expert in some area related to the liturgy. "More common qualities desired in members would be knowledge of liturgy, music, liturgical art and environment, and architecture."[28] Other areas of expertise might include sacramental theology and canon law. Because they serve in the diocesan curia, commission members are appointed by the diocesan bishop.[29]

In addition to stipulating the obligation to keep informed on developments in the liturgy, *Inter oecumenici*, paragraph 47, charges diocesan liturgical commissions with two broad functions: one is advisory; the other is educational. In its advisory capacity, the liturgical commission puts the collective wisdom of its members at the service of the diocesan bishop as he exercises his role as director, promoter, and guardian of the liturgical life in the particular church. Even though the liturgical commission is a purely consultative organ, the bishop should not only make an effort to participate in the group's meetings but do so actively by raising questions about the actual liturgical praxis throughout the diocese and pressing commission members to share freely with him their expertise and the fruit of their own study of issues he has placed

---

27   Sacred Congregation of Rites (Consilium), Instruction *Inter oecumenici*, September 26, 1964, AAS 56 (1964) 887 (DOL 339).

28   Foster, *Liturgical Commissions and Offices*, 60.

29   See Foster, *Liturgical Commissions and Offices*, 61.

before them. Concerning the implementation of the revised *Roman Missal*, the diocesan bishop can benefit greatly by consulting with the liturgical commission about those four areas in IGMR, paragraph 397, where the bishop is competent to establish norms for his diocese. The liturgical commission might profitably be consulted, before any diocesan norms are drafted, to gauge whether or not the particular church would benefit from norms in these areas. If norms are then drafted, the commission should be invited to discuss the proposed text before the norms are promulgated by the bishop. Such a process is time-consuming and labor-intensive. Nevertheless, the quality of the promulgated norms will be greater because of the input given to the bishop by experts whom he trusts and who know the diocese.

While the advice of the liturgical commission is facultative in the above example, such is not the case in IGMR, paragraph 291:

> For the proper construction, restoration, and remodeling of sacred buildings, all who are involved in the work are to consult (*consulant*) the diocesan commission on the Sacred Liturgy and sacred art. The Diocesan Bishop, moreover, should use the counsel and help (*consilio et adiutorio utatur*) of this commission whenever it comes to laying down norms on this matter, approving plans for new buildings, and making decisions on the more important issues.

Not only does the liturgical commission provide guidance to those constructing, renovating, or remodeling churches and oratories, it also gives its learned advice to the diocesan bishop when it comes to establishing norms concerning these issues and approving plans for new buildings.[30]

As important as the liturgical commission's advisory function is, its educational role may be where the commission proves its usefulness. Because the liturgical commission is composed of clerics and lay faithful in the diocese who bring a liturgical or related expertise with them to the table, this group of experts is uniquely qualified to suggest, promote, and provide catechesis on every area of the liturgical apostolate. "The on-going liturgical education of

---

30  While this norm is virtually identical to those in the 1975 and 1969 editions of the IGMR, one change was introduced in 2000. In the present text, the diocesan bishop has replaced the local ordinary as the authority competent to receive the advice of the liturgical commission in laying down norms and approving building plans.

clergy (both presbyters and deacons), the training of lay ministers, and the formation of the Christian faithful are but three broad areas of liturgical education that diocesan commissions can and do provide."[31] The various contacts that members of the commission have (e.g., former professors, colleagues in other dioceses, and professional organizations) serve as a wonderful resource for dioceses to tap when planning a program to implement the revised *Missal*. Whether the diocese needs presenters for workshops on the theological and liturgical meaning of the presidential prayers, people to produce multimedia materials on developments in the liturgical rites or norms, or writers to prepare bulletin inserts on the place of music in the *Missal*, members of the commission not only know whom to contact (and can suggest to the person the specific approach to take in the particular church) but may be able to fill the need themselves.

## Office for Worship

Offices for worship were first mentioned at the universal level in the 1973 *Directory on the Pastoral Ministry of Bishops*.[32] Like the commission for liturgy, the office for worship is a stable and permanent institute in the diocesan curia that, under the authority of the bishop, promotes the liturgical apostolate in the particular church. What distinguishes the office from the commission, however, is the day-to-day presence of the worship office in the diocesan curia: "Unlike liturgical commissions, which meet only periodically, an office for worship is a continuous structure within the diocesan curia. It is this continuity in terms of presence and activity in the particular church that are the liturgy office's greatest strengths."[33]

Like any other ecclesiastical office in the diocese, the office for worship is established by decree of the diocesan bishop (see c. 145). *Promoting Liturgical Renewal*, a 1988 document by the Secretariat for the Bishops' Committee on the Liturgy (now the USCCB Committee on Divine Worship), notes several advantages for establishing a worship office:

---

31    Foster, *Liturgical Commissions and Offices*, 51.

32    Congregation for Bishops, *Directorium de pastorali ministerio episcoporum* (Rome: Typis Polyglottis Vaticanis, 1973), no. 200; English translation from *Directory on the Pastoral Ministry of Bishops*, trans. Benedictine Monks of the Seminary of Christ the King (Mission B.C. Ottawa: Canadian Catholic Conference, 1974), 102.

33    Foster, *Liturgical Commissions and Offices*, 70.

A stable diocesan structure offers the local Church a visible and accessible resource in liturgical matters. Often this results in cooperative efforts with other diocesan offices and agencies, which can result in significant contributions to the life of the diocese. Furthermore, such a liaison eliminates conflicting directives. Obvious examples are liaisons with religious education, adult education, diaconate formation, and so forth. Such a permanent liturgical presence also makes it possible for the diocese to respond in an informed, well-defined, and accessible way to persons having a liturgical concern or question.[34]

Because of the continuous staffing and operation of the office for worship, it is uniquely positioned to execute on the diocesan level the plan to implement the revised *Roman Missal*. Once the diocesan bishop has approved an implementation plan for the entire diocese that has been examined and discussed by the liturgical commission, the office for worship can put the plan into motion, monitor its execution, and respond quickly and effectively to any problems or issues that arise.[35]

## Vicars General and Episcopal

The vicar general and the episcopal vicars are priests who "can carry out all the administrative acts that lie within the competence of the diocesan Bishop, except for those he chooses to reserve to himself and those that the Code of Canon Law *expressly* entrusts to the diocesan Bishop."[36] The diocesan bishop must appoint a vicar general; episcopal vicars may be appointed if the bishop deems it appropriate. Although the executive power of the vicar general is coterminous with the territory of the diocese, the authority of the episcopal vicar extends only to "a certain type of affairs or over the faithful of a specific rite or over certain groups of persons" in the diocese (c. 476). Along with the Roman pontiff and the diocesan bishop and those equivalent to him in law, vicars general and episcopal are also

---

34 USCCB Secretariat for the Bishops' Committee on the Liturgy, *Promoting Liturgical Renewal: Guidelines for Diocesan Liturgical Commissions and Offices of Worship* (Washington, DC: USCCB, 1988), 13.

35 For some reflections on the interrelationship of the diocesan bishop, liturgical commission, and office for worship, see Foster, *Liturgical Commissions and Offices*, 75-83.

36 *Apostolorum successores*, no. 178; emphasis in the original.

local ordinaries (see c. 134 §2). Practically speaking, this means that whenever the law states that the local ordinary may act, the vicar general and those episcopal vicars within whose competence the act falls by reason of issue, rite, or person are also capable to act. However, if the law mentions the diocesan bishop, vicars general and episcopal cannot act in those cases without a mandate from the diocesan bishop (see cc. 134 §3 and 479 §§1-2).

When first promulgated, many of the revised liturgical books granted competence to the local ordinary to act in matters of sacramental and liturgical law. In the weeks prior to the effective date of the revised *Code of Canon Law*, however, the Congregation for the Sacraments and Divine Worship issued a list of emendations to be made in the liturgical books to bring them in line with the new *Code*. In some cases the term "local ordinary" was changed to that of "diocesan bishop," while in others mention of the local ordinary was omitted altogether, thereby giving competence to the diocesan bishop according to canon 838 §4. Despite the restriction of authority in liturgical matters to the diocesan bishop, a mandate can be granted to the vicar general or an episcopal vicar to act in a specific case reserved to the bishop. Nevertheless, such cases should be rare, inasmuch as the diocesan bishop is the principal liturgist for the particular church entrusted to him.

## THE PROCESS OF IMPLEMENTATION

In fulfillment of his supreme pastoral office to shepherd the entire Church, Pope John Paul II approved the third typical edition of the *Missale Romanum* on April 10, 2000. This revised liturgical book for the celebration of the Eucharist contains a revised IGMR as well as (1) the inclusion of Mass texts from ritual celebrations published since 1975; (2) the addition of new Mass texts for a variety of celebrations, including saints added to the universal calendar; (3) changes in some rubrics; and (4) the reordering of some texts.[37] While the revised IGMR was published separately in 2000 "to permit the Bishops to begin preparation of accurate translations of it into the liturgically approved languages and the appropriate forma-

---

37   For an overview of the changes in the revised *Missale Romanum*, see Bishops' Committee on the Liturgy, *Newsletter* 38 (March-April 2002), 61-64.

tion of the clergy and catechesis of the faithful,"[38] the entire *Missale Romanum* was published only in March 2002.

## Unity and Uniformity

Vatican II recognized that "even in the liturgy the Church has no wish to impose a rigid uniformity in matters that do not affect the faith or the good of the whole community."[39] With the breakdown of the notion that unity equals uniformity, challenges have arisen as to the best means of preserving the values that unity and uniformity contribute to the Church. Clearly, unity is more important than uniformity,[40] but uniformity in certain areas can strengthen and manifest unity.

When the Council Fathers called for the revision of all the liturgical rituals, they recognized the advantages that legitimate variations and adaptations offered by respecting and promoting "the genius and talents of the various races and peoples."[41] Thus, the liturgical books that were revised at the Council's direction include a section of possible adaptations to be made by the conference of bishops as well as a section for adaptations to be made by the minister. These are offered in addition to the numerous options provided in the rites themselves for the minister to choose from a number of texts.[42]

It must be acknowledged, however, that all these options—and lack of uniformity—can be a source of consternation for some people. People look to the Church to be a place of stability in a world where change seems to be the only constant. Now, after nearly four decades of praying with an English translation of the *Missal* that has become comfortable, they are being asked to learn new responses and texts. Diocesan bishops and their collaborators are, in many cases, already aware of the problems that the implementation of the revised *Roman*

---

38  Archbishop Francesco Pio Tamburrino, Letter to Bishop Joseph A. Fiorenza, October 31, 2000, quoted in Bishops' Committee on the Liturgy, *Newsletter* 36 (November 2000), in Bishops' Committee on the Liturgy, *Thirty-Five Years of the BCL Newsletter 1965-2000* (Washington, DC: United States Conference of Catholic Bishops, 2004), 1715.

39  SC, no. 37 (DOL 37).

40  The obligation of the Christian faithful to maintain communion with the Church is the first cited in the *Code of Canon Law* (c. 209 §1).

41  SC, no. 37 (DOL 37).

42  See, for example, the three options for the act of penitence (*Missale Romanum*, nos. 426-428) or the choice of Eucharistic Prayers (*Missale Romanum*, nos. 495-521).

*Missal* will cause among the Christian faithful—clergy and laity alike. It will be incumbent on diocesan leaders to help not only those who look forward to the new translation but also those who do not (1) to appropriate for themselves the liturgical principles articulated in *Sacrosanctum Concilium* and subsequent liturgical documents and (2) to acknowledge the right and duty of the Church to order the liturgy, including the celebration of the Eucharist. The revised *Missale Romanum* is but the latest example of this.

A related issue that needs to be acknowledged in the implementation process, if not addressed expressly, is the ecclesiology operative in liturgical law: the Church is a *communio ecclesiarum*. The lay faithful have come to expect differences—even if they have not welcomed them—between parishes in the celebration of the Eucharist. What is harder for people to understand is the fact that neighboring dioceses can—and indeed do—have different liturgical norms. Each diocesan bishop enjoys full authority to shepherd the people entrusted to him as he sees fit, according to the norm of law (see c. 381 §1). In more important matters, the Apostolic See has entrusted to conferences of bishops the competence to make determinations for their dioceses that bind all the bishops in the conference (see c. 455). However, as noted above, "within the limits of his competence, it pertains to the diocesan bishop in the Church entrusted to him to issue liturgical norms which bind everyone" (c. 838 §4). An analogy might be drawn between this ecclesial structure and the civil structure found in the United States. Catholics are bound by universal law, particular law of the conference of bishops, and particular law of their own diocesan bishops, just as those living in the United States are simultaneously bound by federal, state, and municipal laws. While ecclesiastical laws of a lower-level legislator cannot be contrary to a higher law (see c. 135 §2), the particular law of one diocesan bishop may be different from that of a neighboring bishop, much like the laws of one state or city are different from those of its neighbors.

Bishops and their priests exercise their threefold function of teaching, sanctifying, and governing for the service of the Christian faithful entrusted to them. Recognizing the rightful place for variations and different liturgical practices among parishes in a diocese, the bishop and his collaborators will have to wrestle with the question of how to adequately support priests in the process of implementing the *Roman Missal* so that everyone in the diocese can be on the same page.

## The Importance of Catechesis of the Faithful

The first principle and goal for the reform and promotion of the liturgy, articulated in paragraph 14 of *Sacrosanctum Concilium*, is the "full, conscious, and active participation" by the Christian faithful. At the same time, the Council Fathers recognized that "it would be futile to entertain any hopes of realizing this [goal] unless" liturgical catechesis is given to the Christian faithful—both clergy and laity.[43] Indeed, once the pastors had "become thoroughly imbued with the spirit and power of the liturgy,"[44] they were enjoined to "promote the liturgical instruction of the faithful and also their active participation in the liturgy both internally and externally, taking into account their age and condition, their way of life, and their stage of religious development."[45] To the extent that the aforementioned liturgical catechesis was either not done forty years ago or was accomplished only incompletely then, the Church in the United States has another opportunity to provide liturgical formation to the clergy and lay faithful so that all can participate actively in the liturgy, which is their right by virtue of Baptism.

Of course, liturgical catechesis, and specifically catechesis on the *Missale Romanum* (including the IGMR), should be tailored to the particular audiences to whom it is addressed. Clerics—whether priests or deacons, diocesan or religious—should have a solid foundation in the principles for liturgical renewal set forth in *Sacrosanctum Concilium*, since these principles undergird the revision of the rites themselves. With regard to the revised *Roman Missal*, the words of *Sacrosanctum Concilium*, paragraph 18, remain applicable and true: "Priests, both secular and religious, who are already working in the Lord's vineyard are to be helped by every suitable means to understand ever more fully what it is they are doing in their liturgical functions; they are to be aided to live the liturgical life and to share it with the faithful entrusted to their care." As Pope John Paul II observed in his 1992 apostolic exhortation *Pastores dabo vobis*,

---

43  SC, no. 14 (DOL 14).

44  SC, no. 14 (DOL 14).

45  SC, no. 19 (DOL 19).

ongoing formation is imperative throughout a priest's lifetime.[46] While clarified by the theological motivations for ongoing formation,

> there are also purely human reasons which call for the priest to engage in ongoing formation. This formation is demanded by his own continuing personal growth. Every life is a constant path toward maturity, a maturity which cannot be attained except by constant formation. It is also demanded by the priestly ministry seen in a general way and taken in common with other professions, that is, as a service directed to others. There is no profession, job or work which does not require constant updating if it is to remain current and effective. The need to "keep pace" with the path of history is another human reason justifying ongoing formation.[47]

In addition to study days and workshops, ongoing liturgical formation might take place in associations of priests or through various and developing means of social communication. While one cannot discount the many advantages that come from gathering the priests of a diocese or a vicariate together for ongoing formation, neither should one discount using the Internet, including Web-based media—prepared under the guidance of the diocesan bishop and his liturgical experts—for formation when priests cannot easily gather together because of distance or pastoral needs.

The lay faithful are also in need of liturgical formation. Indeed, much of the catechesis prepared for the clergy can be adapted for use with the laity. While lay Catholics today enjoy educational levels not seen by their ancestors, their religious education has not generally kept pace with education in other areas in their lives. This fact ought not to serve as the reason to oversimplify formational materials on the *Missal*. Those charged with preparing catechetical materials for the people in the pew should be encouraged to use various technologies but also to speak in a language the people understand.

Among the faithful, liturgical ministers are in special need of formation on the revised *Roman Missal*. Because liturgical ministers should have already completed some type of basic formation in their respective ministry, they are prepared to delve more deeply

---

46    John Paul II, Apostolic exhortation *Pastores dabo vobis* (Washington, DC: USCCB, 1992), nos. 76-77.

47    *Pastores dabo vobis*, no. 70.

into the values underlying the liturgical norms and rubrics found in the *Missal*. Whether an instituted acolyte or lector, a reader or server, an extraordinary minister of Holy Communion, a minister of music (e.g., cantor, instrumentalist, or choir member), a hospitality minister, or one who cares for the liturgical environment, no liturgical minister should be exempt from participating in this formation process.

In most cases, dioceses are in the best position to prepare various formational materials for liturgical ministers and the people in the pews. Not only will this be a better use of scarce resources, but it will also provide some uniformity between parishes in the diocese as to the liturgical formation that is given. Liturgical catechesis can use a variety of media to instruct the faithful. Bulletin inserts and well-prepared but brief catechetical moments before Mass might work for general formation of the lay faithful, whereas workshops and Web-based materials could prove helpful for liturgical ministers. While it would be inappropriate to make a systematic presentation on the revised *Missal* (as in the form of a lecture) at the homily during Mass, clerics are reminded that a text from the Ordinary or the Proper of the Mass of the day is a suitable source for the homily.[48] Indeed, given the new translation of the Ordinary and Propers in the *Missal*, priests and deacons should consider breaking open these texts for their people.

## The Importance of Presuming Nothing

The publication of the English translation of the third edition of the *Missale Romanum* affords the Christian faithful—both clerics and laity—the opportunity to examine the mindset they bring to the celebration of the Eucharist and their observance of liturgical norms. For this reason, no one should presume to know what the *Roman Missal* says (including the *General Instruction of the Roman Missal* [GIRM] adapted for the dioceses of the United States). Those who preside over and assist at Mass—bishops, presbyters, and deacons— should read carefully the GIRM as well as the text and rubrics of the Ordinary. After reading materials or attending workshops on the revised *Missal*, lay ministers and people in the pew should be encouraged to make a self-examination of their own participation in Mass. Changes have been made not only in the texts proclaimed

---

48   See IGMR, no. 65.

but also in the liturgical norms surrounding them. Two examples will illustrate this point.

First, the 1975 version of the IGMR, paragraph 11, stated the following about introductions made by the priests:

> It is also up to the priest in the exercise of his office of presiding over the assembly to pronounce the instructions and words of introduction and conclusion that are provided in the rites themselves. By their very nature these introductions do not need to be expressed verbatim in the form in which they are given in the Missal; at least in certain cases it will be advisable to adapt them somewhat to the concrete situation of the community.[49]

The parallel norm in the 2002 IGMR, however, has reordered the 1975 norm:

> It is also up to the priest, in the exercise of his office of presiding over the gathered assembly, to offer certain explanations that are foreseen in the rite itself. *Where it is indicated in the rubrics*, the celebrant is permitted to adapt them somewhat in order that they respond to the understanding of those participating.[50]

Second, during the Easter Vigil, the three stations at which the deacon intones *"Lumen Christi"* are different in the revised *Missale Romanum*. In the second typical edition of the *Missal*, the chanted processional dialogue started at the fire, continued at the door of the church, and ended in front of the altar.[51] In the third typical edition of the *Missal*, however, the three stations are at the door of the church, in the middle of the church, and in front of the altar.[52]

These examples illustrate the need for everyone involved in the celebration of the Eucharist to know what is expected of them

---

49   1975 *Institutio Generalis Missalis Romani*, in *Missale Romanum, ex decreto Sacrosancti Oecumenici Concilii Vaticani II instauratum auctoritate Pauli PP. VI promulgatum, editio typica altera* (Vatican City: Libreria Editrice Vaticana, 1975), no. 11 (DOL 1401). The 1975 *Missale Romanum* will hereafter be cited as *Missale Romanum, editio typica altera*.

50   IGMR, no. 31; emphasis added.

51   See the *Vigilia Paschalis* in the 1975 *Missale Romanum, editio typica altera*, nos. 14-15.

52   See the *Vigilia Paschalis* in the 2002 *Missale Romanum, editio typica tertia*, nos. 15-17.

according to the revised *Missal*. It would be wrong to assume that nothing has changed in the new *Missal* except the texts proclaimed.

## Means of Implementation

As noted above, the *Missale Romanum* was published in March 2002. Since the *vacatio legis* had elapsed prior to the book's publication,[53] the norms contained in the IGMR and the rubrics in the *Missale Romanum* itself have been in effect since the book was published. Mindful that most parishes had not obtained copies of the revised *Missale Romanum* and that a reading knowledge of Latin is less widespread among ministers than in previous generations, the secretariat for the USCCB Committee on the Liturgy (now the Committee on Divine Worship) published descriptions of changes in the liturgical rituals for the Chrism Mass and the Easter Triduum in two 2003 issues of its *Newsletter*.[54] Also, with the publication of the *Missale Romanum*, the Latin prayer texts in the book are the only ones that can be used when Mass is celebrated in the Latin language according to the ordinary form. Vernacular translations of these Latin texts can be used only after they have been approved by the conference of bishops and granted the *recognitio* by the Congregation for Divine Worship and the Discipline of the Sacraments (see c. 838 §§2-3)—and then only after the "first use" date given in the decree of promulgation for the vernacular book. This same decree of promulgation will also specify a "must use" date for the new English translation of the *Missal*. After the "must use" date, no previous English translation of the *Missale Romanum* can be used.

In addition to the necessary formation on the liturgical values underlying the *Missal* in general, and ritual norms in particular, diocesan leaders should consider if it is opportune to issue norms

---

53   The *vacatio legis* (literally, "vacation of the law") is the period of time between the law's promulgation by the competent authority and the time the law begins to bind (see c. 8 §1). The purpose of the *vacatio legis* is to give those who will be bound to observe the law time to know the law and prepare for its implementation on the effective date.

   Permission was granted to use the *Missale Romanum* from the time of its publication, but the *editio typica tertia* was required to be used from the Solemnity of the Body and Blood of Christ in 2000 (see Congregation for Divine Worship and the Discipline of the Sacraments, *Decretum de editione typica tertia*, April 20, 2000 [Prot. N. 143/00/L], in *Missale Romanum, editio typica tertia*, 7).

54   For the Easter Vigil, see Bishops' Committee on the Liturgy, *Newsletter* 39 (January 2003): 1-4. For the liturgies on Holy Thursday and Good Friday, see *Newsletter* 39 (March-April 2003): 7-11.

for those competencies that IGMR, paragraph 387, gives to the diocesan bishop. This period also provides an occasion to assess if any other areas of liturgical—and specifically eucharistic—practice need attention: either emphasis or correction. In addressing these issues with the clergy and lay faithful, diocesan leaders often find that persuasion and well-reasoned arguments work better than authoritarian dictates. At the same time, it must be remembered that the law promotes good order and protects the rights of everyone. Because of this, diocesan bishops should not be afraid to issue the appropriate general administrative acts.[55] In addition to general decrees promulgated by the diocesan bishop (see cc. 29-30), the *Code of Canon Law* also provides for general executory decrees (see cc. 31-33) and instructions (see c. 34) as means for local ordinaries to order the celebration of the liturgy in their respective territories. Even if a canonist is not used to assist in drafting the general administrative acts, one should be asked to review the documents to ensure they are congruent with canonical practice. It will be especially important to ensure that diocesan norms are not contrary to universal law or to the particular law of the conference of bishops or the ecclesiastical province (see c. 135 §2).

## IMPLEMENTATION OF THE ROMAN MISSAL IN THE PARISH COMMUNITY

Thus far, our focus has been on the implementation of the *Roman Missal* at the diocesan level. However, the *Missal* will be implemented in each parish community with every celebration of the Eucharist. As noted above, how the pastor, parochial vicars, and visiting priests understand and view the revised *Missal* will have a great impact on how it is received by the people. Priests should make every effort to take the opportunity afforded by the implementation of the *Missal* not only to review and update their own presidential style so that it conforms to the norms and rubrics in the *Missal* but also to review how their parish communities celebrate the Eucharist—on Sundays and weekdays, at ritual events (e.g., marriages and funerals), and at annual celebrations such as the Easter Triduum. Such an examination of liturgical practice can itself be a catechetical tool to implement the revised *Missal* and be

---

55    Likewise, the local ordinary can issue a singular administrative act, e.g., a precept, to a specific person or group of persons should the case require it.

useful for the parish liturgy committee and liturgical ministry coordinators as well as other groups.

Unless the diocesan bishop requires that all parishes and other liturgical assemblies use materials prepared or authorized by the diocese, some parishes might wish to develop their own materials to implement the *Missal*. If this approach is taken, the prudent pastor will have these parish-produced materials reviewed by the diocesan worship office or liturgical commission. Finally, it must be noted that, while the revised *Missal* will provide options for some prayers and rituals, and priests and parishes will develop their own practice concerning these,[56] pastors are not free to introduce practices that are contrary to universal law or to the particular law of the conference of bishops, ecclesiastical province, or diocesan bishop.

# CONCLUSION

There can be little doubt that the implementation of the English translation of the third typical edition of the *Missale Romanum* will be a time of anxiety for many in the Church in the United States. Priests, ministers, and people have to learn new texts and, in some few cases, new rubrics. It is true that liturgical formulas to which American Catholics have grown accustomed in the past forty years will be replaced with new translations. While these old texts possessed ritual value that should be recognized, the introduction of new ones provides an opportunity for the entire Christian assembly to pay attention to what it prays. The Church has long understood that the law of praying establishes the law of believing (*lex orandi, lex credendi*). One danger of the rote recitation of liturgical texts, however, is that priests and people alike no longer attend to the content of what they pray. Until the new texts take on the comfort of a favorite sweater, Catholics in the United States have the occasion to reflect communally and individually on what it is the Church believes when the Lord Jesus unites her to himself—head and members—to worship God.[57]

Americans like to think in terms of programs. For this reason, it has been difficult for some Catholics to speak of the Rite of Christian Initiation of Adults as a *process* rather than a program. Programs are generally linear, having a beginning, a middle, and an

---

56    1983 *Code of Canon Law*, c. 27: "Custom is the best interpreter of laws."

57    SC, no. 7 (DOL 7).

end. Processes, however, are ongoing and spiral-shaped. Similarly, bishops, their liturgical collaborators, and the faithful should resist the temptation to think of the implementation of the revised *Missal* as a program that is complete once the changes it requires have been made. Liturgical catechesis must continue. This is so because the Catholic demographic will continue to change. Catholics from other nations will continue to immigrate to the United States. Lapsed Catholics will return to the practice of the Catholic faith. Younger Catholics will assume an adult place in the Church. All of these groups—and others besides—will need formation in why and how the Church prays as it does. Pastoral leaders would do a disservice to the People of God to make the implementation of the revised *Missal* one more program to be completed instead of an ongoing process in strengthening the liturgical life of the diocesan church. At the same time, it must be recognized that the forms that this ongoing catechesis takes will need adaptation according to the people targeted and the technologies available.

In particular, priests will need continuing liturgical formation and oversight. Such a statement is less an accusation of any ill will on the part of pastors and more an acknowledgment that people, when left to themselves, like to maintain the status quo. As fewer priests must take on increasing responsibilities, they often have little time left for ongoing education or self-reflection on presidential style. Liturgical practices taken for granted can become lifeless. Unchecked abuses harm the *communio* of the Church by violating the rights of the faithful (see c. 214). Rather than an intrusion or power play from above, oversight (i.e., accountability) is a sign of care not only for the liturgy but also for those charged with implementing it in parish communities.

As the 1994 instruction *Varietates legitimae* indicates, the *Missale Romanum*, as translated and adapted for use in the dioceses of the United States, will become part of the organic development of the Roman Rite in its substantial unity.[58] This "new" *Roman Missal* will present challenges in its implementation; at the same time, it will be a gift to the Church in the United States. As a gift, the English translation of the *Missale Romanum, editio typica tertia*, should be implemented in faith and obedience to the Living God manifested through the Church and in service to his people. Pope John Paul II noted in his 2004 apostolic letter *Mane nobiscum Domine*:

---

58   See Congregation for Divine Worship and the Discipline of the Sacraments, Instruction *Varietates legitimae*, 36, January 25, 1994, AAS 87 (1995) 302.

"The Eucharist is a great mystery! And it is one which above all must be *well celebrated.*"[59]

The importance of the *ars celebrandi* was a topic addressed specifically by Pope Benedict XVI in his apostolic exhortation *Sacramentum caritatis*:

> The *ars celebrandi* should foster a sense of the sacred and the use of outward signs which help to cultivate this sense, such as, for example, the harmony of the rite, the liturgical vestments, the furnishings and the sacred space. The eucharistic celebration is enhanced when priests and liturgical leaders are committed to making known the current liturgical texts and norms, making available the great riches found in the *General Instruction of the Roman Missal* and the *Order of Readings for Mass*. Perhaps we take it for granted that our ecclesial communities already know and appreciate these resources, but this is not always the case. These texts contain riches which have preserved and expressed the faith and experience of the People of God over its two-thousand-year history. Equally important for a correct *ars celebrandi* is an attentiveness to the various kinds of language that the liturgy employs: words and music, gestures and silence, movement, the liturgical colors of the vestments. By its very nature the liturgy operates on different levels of communication which enable it to engage the whole human person. The simplicity of its gestures and the sobriety of its orderly sequence of signs communicate and inspire more than any contrived and inappropriate additions. Attentiveness and fidelity to the specific structure of the rite express both a recognition of the nature of Eucharist as a gift and, on the part of the minister, a docile openness to receiving this ineffable gift.[60]

A careful and respectful implementation of the revised *Roman Missal* will not only manifest the *ars celebrandi* but lead to the full, conscious, and active participation of the faithful demanded by

---

59    John Paul II, Apostolic letter *Mane nobiscum Domine*, no. 17, October 7, 2004, AAS 97 (2005) 344; English translation available online at *www.vatican.va/holy_father/john_paul_ii/apost_letters/documents/hf_jp-ii_apl_20041008_mane-nobiscum-domine_en.html*.

60    SacCar, no. 40; English translation from Benedict XVI, *Sacramentum Caritatis* (Washington, DC: USCCB, 2007).

the liturgy.[61] Moreover, in the words of Pope John Paul II, "priests who faithfully celebrate Mass according to the liturgical norms, and communities which conform to those norms, quietly but eloquently demonstrate their love for the Church."[62]

---

61    See SacCar, no. 38.

62    EDE, no. 52.

# CHAPTER 3

# Liturgical Participation of God's People

**VERY REVEREND MARK R. FRANCIS, CSV**

The publication of the new English translation of the third edition of the *Roman Missal* affords Catholics in the United States a unique opportunity to reflect on their liturgical life. Much water has passed under the bridge since the heady days of liturgical reform mandated by the Second Vatican Council and the publication of the first edition of the *Missale Romanum* in 1969. We now face the challenge of introducing a new and somewhat controversial translation. But this challenge cannot be adequately met by attending only to the changes in the words of the Mass or the variations in the rubrics. It is essential that we return to the foundations of the liturgical reform proposed by Vatican II in order to keep these changes in perspective. By their very nature, all vernacular translations are provisory and will need to be revisited due to the dynamic nature of living languages. This is the case especially for a constantly evolving international vernacular like English. At this crucial moment in history, the most constructive thing that we can do is to recall that the very aims of the Council, expressed in the first paragraph of the *Constitution on the Sacred Liturgy* (*Sacrosanctum Concilium*), were intrinsically linked to liturgical renewal:

> This sacred Council has several aims in view: it desires to impart an ever increasing vigor to the Christian life of the faithful; to adapt more suitably to the needs of our own times those institutions which are subject to change; to foster whatever can promote union among all who believe in Christ; to strengthen whatever can help to call the whole of humanity into the household of the Church. The Council

therefore sees particularly cogent reasons for undertaking the reform and promotion of the liturgy.[1]

At the beginning of the twenty-first century, we are now in a position to evaluate how well or how poorly our liturgical ministry has helped to fulfill these desires of the Council Fathers. This moment of opportunity is not unlike the period before the implementation of the new *Missal* in the 1960s. In 1964, anticipating the wide-reaching changes in worship that were about to be experienced by the Church, noted liturgical theologian Romano Guardini spoke of the many "ritual and textual problems" that would inevitably accompany the postconciliar reform.

> The question is whether the wonderful opportunities now open to the liturgy will achieve their full realization, whether we shall be satisfied with just removing anomalies, taking new situations into account, giving better instruction on the meaning of ceremonies and liturgical vessels, or whether we shall relearn a forgotten way of doing things and recapture lost attitudes.[2]

For Guardini, as for many of the pastors and theologians who championed the renewal of Roman Catholic worship, liturgical reform was about more than changing words, rubrical directives, and vestments. It had to do with re-establishing a relationship between the People of God and the liturgy that had been obscured by the passage of time. At its most basic, the goal of the liturgical reform was to enable the baptized to find in the liturgy a source of individual and communal spirituality and thereby rediscover a more traditional appreciation of the Church as the Body of Christ. This process involved re-establishing a relationship of dialogue with the modern world that would necessarily bring about a reassessment and change in Roman Catholic worship, which had remained largely unchanged since the sixteenth century. The revised liturgical books that were promulgated in the late 1960s and early 1970s

---

1   Second Vatican Council, *Sacrosanctum Concilium* (SC), no. 1, in *Documents on the Liturgy 1963-1979: Conciliar, Papal and Curial Texts* (DOL), trans. and ed. International Commission on English in the Liturgy (ICEL) (Collegeville, MN: The Liturgical Press, 1982), 1. Hereafter, quotations of texts in the DOL will include citations to the DOL followed by the margin reference.

2   Romano Guardini, letter written to the organizers of the Third German Liturgical Conference, *Herder Correspondence*, Special Issue (1964): 24-26. Cited by Nathan Mitchell, *Liturgy and the Social Sciences* (Collegeville, MN: The Liturgical Press, 1999), 8.

embodied the program of *aggiornamento*, or updating, outlined in the documents of the Council. The centerpiece of this program was the *Roman Missal*.

This essay will look at the ongoing process of liturgical renewal through the optic of what is arguably the most important and still relevant liturgical principle of the reform: the active participation of God's people in the liturgy. I will first explore the participation of the faithful in the liturgy before and after Vatican II, with special attention to the use of the phrase "active participation" in papal and conciliar teaching. I will then turn to a discussion of *how* participation in the liturgy can be promoted—especially in culturally diverse liturgical assemblies—by focusing on the symbolic nature of Catholic worship, its relationship to culture, and the crucial role of competent liturgical leadership. Another section will be devoted to the various liturgical languages—the ways in which liturgy speaks—with an eye towards active participation. Finally, I will conclude with some observations on the call to conversion—a call inherent in our liturgical worship—that invites all the members of the Church to participation and greater discipleship.

# "ACTIVE PARTICIPATION" OF THE FAITHFUL IN THE LITURGICAL EVENT

The cornerstone of the liturgical renewal was "active participation." This principle was enshrined in *Sacrosanctum Concilium*, paragraph 14, as a fundamental criterion of the Council's program of liturgical reform: "In the reform and promotion of the liturgy . . . full and active participation by all the people is the aim to be considered before all else."[3] Now, almost fifty years after the promulgation of this first document of the Council, it is a good moment to take another look at the history and meaning of this fundamental criterion of the reform. Where did it come from? Has it evolved over the years? Has it been misinterpreted in the implementation of the liturgy called for by Vatican II?

---

3    SC, no. 14 (DOL 14).

# "ACTIVE PARTICIPATION" BEFORE VATICAN II

It would be a mistake to think that the expression "active participation" fell from the sky in 1963 at Vatican II. Quite the contrary: this phrase was first used in relationship to the liturgy by Pope Pius X in his *motu proprio* of 1903 on sacred music, *Tra le solicitudini*. This document was written in Italian and, although it raised the issue of lay participation in the liturgy as a kind of afterthought, *partecipazione attiva* (or as it was later translated into Latin, *participatio actuosa*) became the rallying cry for proponents of the liturgical movement. Toward the end of this document, Pope Pius declared that "the primary and indispensable source" from which the faithful derive "the true Christian spirit [is] active participation in the sacred mysteries and in the public and solemn prayer of the Church."[4] Thus, "active participation" became shorthand used by the leaders of the liturgical movement to sum up their goals of restoring the liturgy to the place it had enjoyed in the early Church: as prayer for all the People of God and as a source for Christian spirituality for laypeople as well as for clergy.

In order to understand how revolutionary Pope Pius's endorsement of "active participation" was at the beginning of the twentieth century, it is necessary to review the role that lay people played in eucharistic worship during the preceding four hundred years. In the late medieval period, prior to the Council of Trent, rubrical commentaries on the Order of Mass still included some mention of lay participation in the liturgy. In his *Ordo Missae* of 1501, Burckard of Strasbourg, master of ceremonies of Pope Alexander VI, presupposes that the faithful participate passively but devoutly in the Rite of Mass. We know this quite simply because the faithful are mentioned from time to time in the text. Among other things, the laity are directed to stand on Sundays and during Eastertide, to answer the prayers at the foot of the altar along with the acolytes, and to

---

4    Pius X, motu proprio *Tra le solicitudini*, November 22, 1903, AAS 36 (1903-1904) 329-339. See Annibale Bugnini, *Documenta pontificia ad instaurationem liturgicam spectantia* (Rome, 1953), 12-13; English translation in R. Kevin Seasoltz, *The New Liturgy: A Documentation 1903 to 1965* (New York: Herder and Herder, 1966), 3-10. Cited in Frederick R. McManus, *Liturgical Participation: On Ongoing Assessment* (Washington, DC: The Pastoral Press, 1988), 4. The original Italian text reads: "*Essendo, infatti, Nostro vivissimo desiderio che il vero spirito cristiano rifiorisca per ogni modo e si mantenga nei fedeli tutti, è necessario provvedere prima di ogni altra cosa alla santità e dignità del tempio, dove appunto i fedeli si radunano per attingere tale spirito dalla sua prima ed indispensabile fonte, che è la* partecipazione attiva *ai sacrosanti misteri e alla preghiera pubblica e solenne della Chiesa*" (emphasis added).

bring up the offerings.[5] Nevertheless, the noted church historian Eamon Duffy describes how the prayer of those in attendance was really different from that of the priest during the Middle Ages:

> The canon of the Mass was recited by the priest in silence . . . so that the people might not be hindered from praying. . . . It was not thought essential or even particularly desirable that the prayer of the laity should be the same as that of the priest at the altar. . . . These were the fundamental requirements for the laity at Mass: to kneel quietly without idle chatter, saying Paters and Aves, to respond to certain key gestures or phrases by changing posture, above all at the sacring to kneel with both hands raised in adoration, to gaze on the Host, and to greet their Lord with an elevation prayer.[6]

It is instructive to note that what little attention the Mass rubrics gave to non-clerics before Trent was entirely suppressed by the introductory matter to the *Missal* of Pius V of 1570: the *Rubricae generales missalis* and the *Ritus Servandus in celebratione Missae.* Due to the polemical atmosphere of the Reformation, the materials treated lay participation at Mass as non-essential in order to insist that the eucharistic sacrifice was validly celebrated by the priest alone. Because of this focus on the necessity of the priestly role at the Eucharist, Roman authorities continued to look with suspicion on lay participation at Mass well into the nineteenth century. Using a translation to follow along with the Latin prayers of the priest was long discouraged. Some vernacular translations of the ordinary of

---

5    *Ordo servandus per sacerdotum in celebratione Missae sine cantu et sine ministris secundum ritum S. Romanae Ecclesiae;* see Burkhard Neunheuser, "The Liturgies of Pius V and Paul VI," in *Roles of the Liturgical Assembly* (New York: Pueblo, 1977), 208; John K. Leonard and Nathan Mitchell, *The Postures of the Assembly During the Eucharistic Prayer* (Chicago: Liturgy Training Publications, 1994), 72-74. See also a mention of this document by Nathan Mitchell and John Baldovin, "*Institutio Generalis Missalis Romani* and the Class of Liturgical Documents to Which It Belongs," in *A Commentary on the General Instruction of the Roman Missal*, eds. Edward Foley et al. (Collegeville, MN: The Liturgical Press/Pueblo, 2007), 20-21. Adrien Nocent has pointed out that the lack of attention to the role of non-clerics in the Rite of Mass is also due to the fact that the model for both Burckard's *Ordo* and the subsequent *Missal* of Pius V was the practice of the papal court codified in the *Missal* of the Roman Curia of 1474. See Nocent, *La Messa prima e dopo San Pio V* (Casale Monferrato: Piemme, 1985), 45-52.

6    Eamon Duffy, *The Stripping of the Altars: Traditional Religion in England 1400-1580* (New Haven, CT: Yale University Press, 1992), 117.

the Mass were even placed on the Church's *Index Librorum Prohibitorum* (*Index of Forbidden Books*). As Gerard Ellard points out:

> As late as 1851 and again in 1857, the Holy See refused to allow liturgical translations in the vernacular, even as a tool for the laity in greater appreciation of the Mass: "It is not permitted to translate the Ordinary of the Mass . . . into the vernacular, and print the same for use of the faithful, nor can such a work get the approbation of the Bishop" (June 6, 1857).[7]

In 1877 Pope Pius IX reversed this decision and allowed any bishop to authorize the publication of vernacular hand missals for lay people. It was finally Pope Leo XIII (1878-1903) who regularized the publication of such resources, requiring only an imprimatur from the local bishop. This underlines the fact that, despite some current ahistorical nostalgia, seeing the Mass liturgy as a source for lay prayer—even in translation—is a relatively recent development.[8]

All of the foregoing helps to place Pope Pius X's call for "active participation" of the laity in greater relief. This call was repeated by his successor, Pius XI, in another document on liturgical music published in 1928. He encouraged lay people to sing Gregorian chant, affirming the principle that "it is most important . . . when the faithful assist at the sacred ceremonies . . . [that] they should not be merely detached and silent spectators, but filled with a deep sense of the beauty of the liturgy, should sing alternately with the clergy or the choir, as it is prescribed."[9]

In many ways these papal exhortations to lay involvement in worship served to legitimize the work of the liturgical movement. Key leaders of the movement in Europe and America who had agitated for lay participation felt vindicated. To name just two of these pioneers: Dom Lambert Beauduin (1873-1960), of the Monastery Mont César in Belgium, tried to create a bridge between Christian lay people and the liturgy; and Dom Virgil Michel (1890-1938), monk of St. John's Abbey in Collegeville, Minnesota, and the American founder of *Orate Fratres* (later *Worship*), popularized much of

---

7   Gerald Ellard, *The Mass of the Future* (Milwaukee: Bruce Publishing Company, 1948), 30, cited by Keith F. Pecklers in *Dynamic Equivalence: The Living Language of Christian Worship* (Collegeville, MN: Liturgical Press/Pueblo, 2003), 30.

8   On the historic vicissitudes of lay participation in the liturgy, especially in regard to the use of the vernacular, see Pecklers's engaging treatment in *Dynamic Equivalence*, 1-41.

9   Pius XI, Apostolic constitution *Divini cultus*, December 20, 1928, AAS 21 (1929) 33-41; English translation in Seasoltz, *The New Liturgy*, 58-63.

European liturgical scholarship by insisting that lay people "should pray the Mass, not just pray during Mass."

Active participation, though, received its most considered support before Vatican II from Pope Pius XII in his encyclical on the liturgy, *Mediator Dei* (1947). Building on his previous encyclical *Mystici Corporis* (1942), where he had re-proposed the Pauline notion of the Church as the Mystical Body of Christ, *Mediator Dei* speaks eloquently of the liturgy as the public worship "rendered by the Mystical Body of Christ in the entirety of its Head and members."[10]

Pope Pius XII presents the notion of participation in worship as both exterior and interior. It is exterior because worship is an incarnated activity or, as the Pope puts it, "because the nature of man as a composite of body and soul requires it to be so."[11] It is interior insofar as the end of the liturgy is our transformation in Christ. Pius XII insists that the "chief element of divine worship must be interior. For we must always live in Christ and give ourselves to Him completely, so that in Him, with Him and through Him the heavenly Father may be duly glorified."[12] Importantly, though, the Pope maintains that it is a mistake to overly contrast the exterior dimensions of participation with the interior, because the "sacred liturgy requires . . . that both of these elements [exterior and interior] be intimately linked with each other. This recommendation the liturgy itself is careful to repeat, as often as it prescribes an exterior act of worship. . . . Otherwise religion clearly amounts to mere formalism, without meaning and without content."[13]

Following on the heels of *Mediator Dei*, the liturgies of Holy Week were revised, and experiments were promoted for the so-called dialogue Mass in which the priest celebrant would pray the prayers in an audible voice and the people would answer the responses with the acolytes. It would be a mistake, however, to overestimate the

---

10  Pius XII, Encyclical *Mediator Dei*, no. 24, December 2, 1947, AAS 39 (1947) 521-600; for the English translation, as well as reference numbers not present in the original Latin text, visit the Web site of the Holy See: *www.vatican.va/holy_father/pius_xii/encyclicals/documents/hf_p-xii_enc_20111947_mediator-dei_en.html.*

11  *Mediator Dei*, no. 23.

12  *Mediator Dei*, no. 24.

13  *Mediator Dei*, no. 24.

effect all this had on the worship life of the average parish. As Msgr. Frederick McManus, who lived through these times, describes it:

> active liturgical participation before Vatican II was a genuine and vigorous reality, but only in those places and churches where the ordained and lay promoters of the liturgical movement had their limited impact. . . . The call of the successive bishops of Rome for participation by the whole people was perhaps heard as little as the message of their social encyclicals.[14]

Interestingly, according to *Mediator Dei*, one of the key factors that impeded active participation of the laity in the Mass was the inability of many lay people to understand and enter into liturgical prayer. Despite the great advance represented by this encyclical, Pope Pius XII simply accepted the fact that the liturgy, even in translation, was not able to be the prayer of all the people:

> Many of the faithful are unable to use the Roman missal even though it is translated in the vernacular; nor are all capable of understanding correctly the liturgical rites and formulas. So varied and diverse are men's talents and characters that it is impossible for all to be moved and attracted to the same extent by community prayers, hymns and liturgical services.[15]

The Pope went on to suggest that these lay people can participate in the Mass and obtain its spiritual fruits through other means such as devotional prayers—as long as such prayers are in harmony with the sacred rites: "They can adopt some other method which proves easier for certain people; for instance, they can lovingly meditate on the mysteries of Jesus Christ or perform other exercises of piety or recite prayers which, though they differ from the sacred rites, are still essentially in harmony with them."[16]

While *Mediator Dei* marked a real way forward in promoting lay participation in the liturgy, the presupposition underlying its discussion of active participation was that the *Ordo Missae* in Latin was not to be changed, even though the rite was not accessible to

---

14    McManus, *Liturgical Participation*, 5.

15    *Mediator Dei*, no. 108.

16    *Mediator Dei*, no. 108.

all people. If lay people wished to participate more fully in worship, they were to learn Latin or at least follow the celebration in translation. For that reason, *Mediator Dei* had to propose a kind of secondary devotional way to assist at Mass, calling it a kind of participation for those lay people for whom Latin and even literacy were obstacles.

## ACTIVE PARTICIPATION AND SACROSANCTUM CONCILIUM

*Sacrosanctum Concilium* (*Constitution on the Sacred Liturgy*) takes the teachings of Pius X, Pius XI, and Pius XII on active participation to their logical conclusion. Roughly one-third of its 131 articles are concerned with promoting the active participation of the assembly in the liturgy. The key paragraph of the constitution calls for *all the faithful* to be led to "that full, conscious and active participation in liturgical celebrations called for by the very nature of the liturgy. Such participation by the Christian people as 'a chosen race, a royal priesthood, a holy nation, God's own people' (1 Pt 2:9) is their right and duty by reason of their baptism."[17]

It is noteworthy that, unlike *Mediator Dei, Sacrosanctum Concilium* does not equivocate regarding the active participation of *all* the faithful in the liturgy. It is their right and duty because of the dignity of their Baptism, which deputes them to worship.[18] Moreover, it is also an ecclesial action containing "rich instruction for the faithful."[19] In order for the liturgy to be understood and become real communal prayer of the gathered Church, the Council Fathers realized that the Tridentine liturgy itself needed to be reformed. The way was opened for a wider use of the vernacular to make worship accessible to all the faithful.[20] The very structure of the rites themselves needed to be changed so as to facilitate active participation: "In this reform both texts and rites should be so drawn up that they express more clearly the holy things they signify and that the Christian people, as far as possible, are able to understand them with ease and to take part in the rites fully, actively, and as befits a community."[21]

---

17  SC, no. 14 (DOL 14).

18  See Second Vatican Council, *Lumen gentium*, no. 11, and McManus, *Liturgical Participation*, 10, especially note 19.

19  SC, no. 33 (DOL 33); on worship as ecclesial action, see also SC, nos. 26, 41, and 42.

20  See SC, no. 35 §2.

21  SC, no. 21 (DOL 21); see also SC, no. 34.

How, then, is active participation described in *Sacrosanctum Concilium*? Both aspects of participation noted by *Mediator Dei*—exterior and interior—are specifically mentioned as being part of "active participation." The nature of this participation is further described in a later paragraph of *Sacrosanctum Concilium*, which enumerates the forms that participation can take: "To promote active participation, the people should be encouraged to take part by means of acclamations, responses, psalmody, antiphons, and songs, as well as by actions, gestures, and bearing. And at the proper times all should observe a reverent silence."[22]

It is significant that in addition to these external forms of participation—verbal and non-verbal—for the first time in the history of the Roman Rite, reverent silence is called for as a form of active participation. It is a misunderstanding, then, to think that *Sacrosanctum Concilium* uses this expression to promote a kind of mindless activism in the liturgy on the part of the faithful.[23]

It is also important to note that *Sacrosanctum Concilium*, by stating its preference for communal over private celebrations, specifies that the reformed rites are to make "provision for communal celebrations involving the presence and active participation of the faithful."[24] Liturgy is most fully expressive of the nature of the Church when the baptized are convoked in an assembly hierarchically constituted around the bishop, with members of the assembly participating according to their particular role.[25] The various liturgical ministries are all ordered to serve the assembly and to facilitate the participation of the faithful.[26] While all are members of the assembly, including the ordained ministers, all have particular functions to perform. Therefore, "active participation" does not mean that everyone does or says the same thing at the same time.

---

22    SC, no. 30 (DOL 30).

23    F. R. McManus, "The Goal Remains Active Participation, Active Sharing," *Pastoral Music* (June-July, 1998): 18.

24    SC, no. 27 (DOL 27).

25    See SC, nos. 41, 26.

26    See SC, no. 29; see also Mark R. Francis, "The Liturgical Assembly," in *Fundamental Liturgy: Handbook for Liturgical Studies*, ed. Anscar Chupungco (Collegeville, MN: The Liturgical Press, 1998), 129-143, especially 139-141.

## PROMOTING ACTIVE PARTICIPATION AFTER VATICAN II

In the years following the Council, the need to promote the full, conscious, and active participation of God's people in worship was expressed time and again in subsequent instructions by the Holy See and in the reformed liturgies themselves—both in the texts and rubrics of the rites as well as in their *praenotanda* or introductions. The immediate embrace of the vernacular by bishops' conferences reflected the enthusiasm with which the principle of active participation was received. While speaking at an Angelus blessing in St. Peter's Square on March 7, 1965, Pope Paul VI remarked that the use of the vernacular had been judged by the Church "to be necessary to make its prayer understandable and grasped by all. The good of the faithful calls for this kind of action, making possible their active share in the Church's public worship." Speaking to the people gathered in the square, he went on to say that the introduction of the vernacular "means you, the faithful, so that you may be able to unite yourselves more closely to the Church's prayer, [and] pass over from being simple spectators to becoming active participants."[27] Although subsequent pronouncements by the Roman authorities have continued to support active participation, two principal concerns have been voiced. The first is that this participation not be understood as merely external. Some have even suggested that the English adjective "active" was a mistranslation of what is meant by "*actuosa*" in Latin, implying that the Council had a much more passive, interior mode of participation in mind and that this intention was misinterpreted by both the Consilium who drafted the renewed rites and the bishops' conferences that implemented them. While few would deny that the implementation of the renewed rites has been uneven, it is inaccurate to say that "active participation" was misinterpreted by the framers of the renewed liturgy. As we have seen from the use of the phrase by Pius X, "active participation" in the liturgy as "the primary and indispensable source from which the faithful are to derive the true Christian spirit" has always included both the internal and external dimensions.[28] Pope Benedict XVI has helpfully emphasized that "the active participation called for by the Council must be understood in more substantial terms, on the basis

---

27  Paul VI, Remarks at the Angelus to the people in St. Peter's Square, on the beginning of the vernacular in the liturgy, March 7, 1965 (DOL 399).

28  See also SC, no. 14, and McManus's commentary on the adjective "active" in "The Goal Remains Active Participation, Active Sharing," 19.

of a greater awareness of the mystery celebrated and its relationship to daily life."[29] This assertion does not, however, necessarily make "internal participation" and "external participation" mutually exclusive. As we have seen, linking these two dimensions of participation was an important insight of Pius XII in *Mediator Dei*.

A second, related concern involves safeguarding the role of the priest celebrant in the liturgy, by preventing confusion between the ministerial priesthood and the royal priesthood of all believers. This difference, emphasized in *Mediator Dei* and *Lumen gentium*, has been made even more emphatic in the 2002 revision of the *General Instruction of the Roman Missal* (GIRM) and in Pope Benedict's apostolic exhortation *Sacramentum caritatis*.[30] However, it also needs to be emphasized that both "priesthoods"—lay and ordained—participate in the one priesthood of Jesus Christ. It is upon this priesthood, linked by Baptism, that any involvement in the liturgy on the part of both ordained and lay is founded.

As we face the challenge today of continuing the liturgical renewal set in motion by the Council, how can we promote the full, conscious, and active participation of the assembly called for by *Sacrosanctum Concilium*? This call needs to be understood not as a kind of mindless activity; rather, it needs to look at the liturgy itself as "the primary and indispensable source from which the faithful derive the true Christian spirit." In order to face this challenge competently, we need to reflect on who we are gathering, and especially on the cultural context of our assemblies. We then need to cultivate a profound confidence in the ability of our liturgical tradition—through sign and symbol—to unite us as members of the Body of Christ and transcend all that divides us. Moreover, greater attention to what the bishops' Synod on the Eucharist called the *ars celebrandi*—or "art of celebrating"—will help all of us enter into the liturgical celebration more profoundly and enable us to make the connections between worship and our ethical lives.

---

29  Benedict XVI, Post-synodal apostolic exhortation *Sacramentum caritatis* (SacCar) (Washington, DC: United States Conference of Catholic Bishops [USCCB], 2007), no. 52.

30  See *Lumen gentium*, no. 10. Pope Benedict XVI, in SacCar, no. 53, emphasizes the need to respect the distinct hierarchical roles in the assembly since "the beauty and the harmony of the liturgy find eloquent expression in the order by which everyone is called to participate actively." There is still a need, however, to relate the hierarchical priesthood with the royal priesthood of the whole Church in a more satisfactory way. See David Power and Catherine Vincie, "Theological and Pastoral Reflections," in *A Commentary on the General Instruction of the Roman Missal*, 52-55.

# LITURGY, PARTICIPATION, AND CULTURE

An important aspect of the active participation of God's people in the liturgy is the cultural context in which the celebration takes place. This concern was enshrined in *Sacrosanctum Concilium*, paragraphs 37-40, and was further refined in 1994 by *Varietates legitimae*, the fourth instruction on inculturation and the Roman liturgy.[31] Concern regarding the ongoing need for inculturation as a *sine qua non* for active participation has continued. As Pope Benedict noted in his exhortation on the Eucharist, the participants at the recent Synod on the Eucharist "frequently stressed the importance of the active participation of the faithful in the eucharistic sacrifice. In order to foster this participation, provision may be made for a number of adaptations appropriate to different contexts and cultures."[32] Inculturation, though originally viewed in *Sacrosanctum Concilium* as a missionary concern, is now seen a matter that affects the whole Church. The need for inculturation was voiced during all of the continental bishops' synods held in Rome (Africa, America, Asia, Oceania, and Europe) and was further discussed in the subsequent papal exhortations that followed each of these synods.

It is significant that it was thought necessary in 2002 to add a whole new chapter to the *General Instruction of the Roman Missal* entitled "Adaptations Within the Competence of Bishops and Bishops' Conferences."[33] This chapter describes the Roman Rite's relationship to culture as dynamic. It notes that "throughout the ages, the Roman Rite has not only preserved the liturgical usages that arose in the city of Rome, but has also in a deep, organic, and harmonious way incorporated into itself certain other usages derived from the customs and culture of different peoples and of various particular Churches of both West and East."[34] This acknowledgment of the ongoing influence of culture on Catholic worship is also

---

31  Congregation for Divine Worship and the Discipline of the Sacraments, Instruction *Varietates legitimae* (VL) (Fourth Instruction for the Right Implementation of the *Constitution on the Sacred Liturgy* of the Second Vatican Council), March 24, 1994. Available at the FDLC Web site at *www.fdlc.org/Liturgy_Resources/Liturgy_Documents_files/LITURGYVeritatesLegitimae.htm*.

32  SacCar, no. 54.

33  For a commentary on this chapter of the *General Instruction of the Roman Missal* (nos. 386-399) see Mark Francis and Gary Neville, "Adaptations Within the Competence of Bishops and Bishops' Conferences," in *A Commentary on the General Instruction of the Roman Missal*, 447-467.

34  *General Instruction of the Roman Missal* (GIRM) (Washington, DC: USCCB, 2003), no. 397.

affirmed by *Varietates legitimae*: "During the course of the centuries, the Roman rite has known how to integrate texts, chants, gestures and rites from various sources and to adapt itself in local cultures in mission territories."[35] As vernacular translations are produced from the typical editions of the liturgical books (which are themselves cultural products), this traditional openness of the Roman Rite to new influences needs to continue "so the liturgy of the church must not be foreign to any country, people or individual, and at the same time it should transcend the particularity of race and nation."[36] For the Church in the United States, the Roman Rite—even in this new translation—must remain in dialogue with U.S. culture in order to be able to speak intelligibly to modern Catholics.

While inculturation of the liturgy is a basic way to promote the active participation of the assembly at worship, the fact that the United States is becoming more and more multicultural presents a new set of challenges to our worship.[37] *Varietates legitimae* underlines the fact that "in the countries with a long standing Western Christian tradition . . . the measures of adaptation envisaged in the liturgical books were considered on the whole sufficient to allow for legitimate local diversity." Yet it may be necessary to go beyond these measures in countries "where several cultures coexist, especially as a result of immigration."[38] Given the multicultural reality that touches the worship life of an ever-increasing number of our parishes in the United States, adaptations to the rites in order to foster full, conscious, and active participation within culturally diverse assemblies is a growing pastoral concern that cannot be ignored.[39]

The Pontifical Council for Pastoral Care of Migrants and Itinerant People[40] and the United States Conference of Catholic Bish-

---

35 VL, no. 17; see a parallel passage in the GIRM, no. 397.

36 VL, no. 18.

37 "Minorities, now roughly one-third of the U.S. population, are expected to become the majority in 2042, with the nation projected to be 54 percent minority in 2050. By 2023, minorities will comprise more than half of all children" (U.S. Census Bureau, Press Release, August 14, 2008, *www.census.gov/Press-Release/www/releases/archives/population/012496.html*).

38 VL, no. 7.

39 VL, no. 49, is dedicated to considerations of multicultural worship and warns of certain dangers, such as folklorism and the politicization of the liturgy, that could inappropriately instrumentalize the community's worship to celebrate a given culture over others.

40 Pontifical Council for Pastoral Care of Migrants and Itinerant People, Instruction *Erga migrantes caritas Christi* (*The Love of Christ Towards Migrants*), *www.vatican.va/roman_curia/pontifical_councils/migrants/documents/rc_pc_migrants_doc_20040514_erga-migrantes-caritas-christi_en.html*.

ops[41] have both spoken of the specific challenges of multicultural communities and the special factors that need to be considered in promoting active participation in the worship life of the parish. Local churches, in welcoming immigrant groups, need to develop approaches to liturgical catechesis and sacramental preparation that are geared to the cultures of the new groups and are respectful of their traditional values. These documents make the connection time and again between participation in the liturgy and participation in the life of the local church.[42]

While official liturgical documents acknowledge the challenge of multicultural communities, they have not included much practical advice about how to bring together people from a variety of cultures and languages into one liturgical assembly.[43] After decades of experience, however, the goal of ministry in multicultural parishes is becoming clearer. There seems to be a growing consensus among both bishops and pastoral agents to move from a multicultural approach, where various cultural groups coexist in the same parish, to an intercultural approach, where the cultural groups of the parish actively work in harmony and are in ongoing communication and mutual sharing.[44] This intercultural sensitivity is aptly and prophetically summed up in the pastoral letter of black bishops of the United States, *What We Have Seen and Heard*: "To be Catholic is to be universal. To be universal is not to be uniform. It does mean that the gifts of individuals and of particular groups become the common heritage shared by all."[45]

Just how the particular gifts of each group become the "common heritage shared by all" is the challenge of inculturation and ministry in a multicultural community. It suggests that more than ever before, rather than arriving on the scene with preconceived

---

41    Most importantly, see USCCB, *Welcoming the Stranger Among Us* (Washington, DC: USCCB, 2000).

42    See *Erga migrantes caritas Christi*, no. 44.

43    Among the various resources currently available for ministering liturgically in communities with two or more cultural groups is my short monograph sponsored by the FDLC, *Multicultural Celebrations: A Guide* (Washington, DC: FDLC, 2002); see also Cardinal Roger Mahony, "The Challenge and Blessing of Many Cultures," in "Gather Faithfully Together: A Guide for Sunday Mass," *Origins* 27:15 (September 25, 1997): 245. On preaching, see Archbishop Wilton Gregory's insightful presentation "Preaching in the Multicultural Context of the U.S.", *Origins* 37:33 (January 31, 2008): 521-526.

44    See Robert Schreiter, "Pastoral Leadership: Moving into the Future," *Origins* 38:2 (May 22, 2008). See especially 25, 26. See also USCCB, *Welcoming the Stanger Among Us*, 34-36.

45    *What We Have Seen and Heard: A Pastoral Letter on Evangelization from the Black Bishops of the United States* (Cincinnati, OH: St. Anthony Messenger Press, 1984), 4.

opinions and solutions, pastoral agents need to open themselves to the people in their local churches to discover and help facilitate the sharing of gifts among sisters and brothers of different cultures. This has profound implications for liturgical ministry, which will be discussed below.

Culture is not, however, the only thing that divides our assemblies and renders active participation difficult. Even monocultural parishes and assemblies are divided by other factors that need to be taken into account in trying to make the liturgy a real source of spirituality for the assembled people of God. As the United States Conference of Catholic Bishops (USCCB) described in its document on preaching, *Fulfilled in Your Hearing*:

> The Eucharistic assembly that gathers Sunday after Sunday is a rich and complex phenomenon. Even in parishes that are more or less uniform in ethnic, social, or economic background, there is great diversity: men and women, old and young, the successes and the failures, the joyful and the bereaved, the fervent and the halfhearted, the strong and the weak.[46]

Culture, language, educational level, economic class, gender, age, personal conditions, and psychology all affect the way that the members of the assembly will be able to participate in a full, conscious, and active way in worship. Whether it be in preaching, in catechesis, or in liturgy preparation, awareness of the situation of the assembly is a crucial factor in fostering participation of all in both the liturgy and the life of the parish in general.

Because Catholic worship is grounded in Christ and communicates symbolically, our liturgy is capable both of expressing a diversity of cultural approaches to the faith as well as of transcending these very differences. In order for this to be possible, though, we need to respect the way our Catholic tradition of worship communicates the world-transforming power of God in the Paschal Mystery. We need to realize that the Paschal Mystery paradoxically uses our very diversity to unite us in Christ. As Peter Fink has pointed out:

> On the one hand, diversity is a necessary condition for unity; any relationship that does not tolerate and even rev-

---

46   USCCB Committee on Priestly Life and Ministry, *Fulfilled in Your Hearing: The Homily in the Sunday Assembly* (Washington, DC: USCCB, 1982), 5.

erence diversity is not communion at all. On the other hand, diversity is a necessary condition for holding otherness in reverence. We must see diversity from within communion and see communion from within diversity.[47]

In a practical way, how can diversity bring us into unity in the context of liturgy? How can reverence for diversity aid us in promoting active participation of all the members of our assemblies? In order to propose some answers to these important questions, we need to reflect on how liturgy speaks.

# ACTIVE PARTICIPATION AND THE LANGUAGES OF THE LITURGY

## WORDS AT WORSHIP

Much of the controversy that has arisen over the new English translation of the *Roman Missal* is about words. We have grown used to a certain version of our prayers, and any change in prayer texts makes most of us uneasy. While much could be said of the problematic aspects of the new translation, we are left with the question, How can we promote active participation in light of these new texts?

At this point it is helpful to review our use of words in the liturgy: the words of the priest celebrant, the prayers of the faithful, and the other unscripted words that frame the texts found in the *Roman Missal*. All of these can be considered liturgical speech. How does such speech function in the context of worship?

First of all, liturgical speech is not the discourse of the classroom. It is not technically doctrinal, concerned with explaining the Trinity or delving into scholastic philosophical categories. It should lead all present to an awareness of God's presence and incite in all thanksgiving and love for our redemption in Christ. As Robert Hovda has said so well:

There is a modest and essential place in every liturgical celebration for human rhetoric, but it is a modest place, subordinate to the proclamation of the word of God in scripture, subordinate to the symbolic action of the whole assembly.

---

47    Peter Fink, "Eucharist as a Call to Unity," *Liturgical Ministry* 17 (2008): 105.

Implied in all this is the conviction that what is most important about public worship is that we gather the sisters and
brothers together for a festival, a special occasion, a celebration of the reign of God. . . . A celebration of the reign
of God that goes way beyond the tight, drab, rationalistic,
verbose, pedagogical exercises we sometimes try to make
of it.[48]

One of the most trenchant critiques of the new liturgy is that it is
wordy. In addition to the "scripted" texts—the Scripture reading, the
presidential prayers of the priest celebrant—assemblies are sometimes bombarded by frequent and long-winded explanations of the
"theme" of the Mass that become little homilies given throughout
the celebration. To top it off, the Mass often concludes with long
announcements that repeat what is printed in the parish bulletin.
Much of this verbal communication also takes place without pause or
silence. The cumulative effect of this verbal avalanche is to create an
atmosphere where the words themselves lose their ability to speak,
to communicate. This is especially true in multicultural assemblies
whose members may not all have a good grasp of English—or of
any other language in which the liturgy is being celebrated.

Attention to rhythm, cadence, volume, emphasis, is basic to oral
communication. The same is also true of body language and emotional involvement that accompanies the words. A priest celebrant
saying "The Lord be with you" while paging through the *Missal* with
his head in the book should not be surprised if he elicits a lacklus-
ter response from those present. It is also important to distinguish
between the various levels or genres of language used in worship.
Consider greetings and acclamations. The stylized nature of a liturgical greeting and response at the beginning of Mass does not make
it insincere; it signals that what we are about is of a different order
than other social activity. It establishes a ritual moment. The acclama-
tory nature of the Holy, Holy or the Great Amen accompanying the
Eucharistic Prayer are meant to be full-throated communal expressions of praise appropriately set to music, rather than perfunctory,
mumbled responses incapable of expressing joy or conviction. Proc-
lamations, such as the reading of the Scripture, in addition to being
easily heard and understood, should be delivered in such a way that
the faith of the individual reader and his or her knowledge of what is

---

48    Robert Hovda, "Vesting of Liturgical Ministers," *Worship* 54 (March 1980), cited in Gabe Huck
      (ed.), *A Sourcebook About Liturgy* (Chicago: Liturgy Training Publications, 1994), 1.

being read shines forth. Finally, because of the complicated sentence structure and unusual vocabulary of the new translation, the texts of the *Missal*—the Collects as well as Eucharistic Prayers—require more preparation on the part of the priest celebrant. If the Scriptures in the Lectionary or the prayers of the *Roman Missal* are not understood by the one speaking them, this verbal communication will be met with incomprehension and boredom.

## BEYOND THE VERBAL

With the introduction of the new translation of the *Roman Missal*, it is natural to fixate on the differences in the wording of the prayer texts and the people's responses. Many of these changes need to be the focus of catechesis in order to be properly understood. Nevertheless, if we limit ourselves to dealing with the verbal changes in the texts of the Mass, we will be missing an important opportunity to attend to what ultimately is a more effective way to promote active participation: the whole of our liturgical and sacramental tradition itself, which has always gone beyond the verbal.

While language is important, we come into the very presence of God with our bodies as well as our minds. Nathan Mitchell, with his characteristic eloquence, speaks about how our liturgical tradition itself is both embodied and inherently multicultural:

> *Sacrosanctum Concilium* reminds us that Catholic worship is, by definition, "multi-cultural"; that liturgy flows not from words alone, but from "*ritus . . . et preces . . . et sacram actionem*," i.e., from "rituals and prayers and sacred deeds or actions." The Roman liturgy's original "native tongue" was thus neither Greek nor Latin; it was—and remains—a language of the body; a language both *personal* and *corporate*; a language *sung* as "sound" and *danced* as "ritual"; a language of light and fragrance and motion; and language of song and ceremony and silence. Liturgy's "native tongue" is *doxology*, and doxology must always be *embodied*, not only as "thoughts" or "words" or "formulas," but as the *hands* lifted in jubilation or praise; as the *arms* stretched out in supplication; as the *feet* of a pilgrim people in procession; as the *knee* bent in penance and supplication; as the *whole torso* bowed in awe and adoration. Liturgy's "native tongue"

is the speech of oil and water, fire and salt, bread and wine, washing and anointing, eating and drinking, touching and blessing. In a word, liturgy's "native tongue" is our *bodily life* and the language of Christian "doxology" is inevitably a language of flesh and blood.[49]

Reflecting on the embodied way that liturgy communicates helps to point us to a more profound respect for the symbolic nature of our worship and offers an important insight into promoting participation. As *Sacrosanctum Concilium* affirms: "In the liturgy, by means of signs perceptible to the senses, human sanctification is signified and brought about in ways proper to each of these signs."[50] A key phrase here is "perceptible to the senses." We come into the presence of the sacred with our bodies—not just our minds. For this reason Catholic liturgy, like Orthodox Christian worship, insists on the importance of all our senses at communal prayer. It is with our senses as well as our minds that we engage symbol. Our bodies are—our physicality is—thus the medium not only by which we engage in worship, but also upon which our spirituality is based and through which we enter into relationship with God.[51] Our worship is so dependent on our "bodiliness" that the noted French sacramental theologian Jean-Louis Chauvet insightfully subtitled his book on the Sacraments "The Word of God at the Mercy of the Body."[52]

Symbols, as they are used in the liturgy, communicate in a very different way than does a mathematical equation or the instructions on how to assemble a bicycle. A symbol, as Mitchell points out, is both personal and corporate, and for that reason it can mean a range of things simultaneously. Take the example of the paschal candle. At the Easter Vigil, after the Easter fire is blessed and the candle is lighted outside the entrance to the church, the candle is introduced into a darkened assembly by the chant "The Light of Christ" and

---

49    Nathan Mitchell, "Response to the Conference by Father Juan Javier Flores, OSB," given at Languages of Worship/El lenguaje de la liturgia Conference, June 16-19, 2003, University of Notre Dame. Cited by Raúl Gómez in Introduction, *Languages of Worship/El lenguaje de la liturgia* (Chicago: Liturgy Training Publications, 2004), 5.

50    SC, no. 7 (DOL 7).

51    See the provocative and insightful essay by James Empereur, "The Physicality of Worship," in *Bodies of Worship: Exploration in Theory and Practice*, ed. Bruce T. Morrill (Collegeville, MN: The Liturgical Press, 1999), 137-155.

52    Louis-Marie Chauvet, *Les sacrements. Parole de Dieu au risque du corps* (Paris: Les Éditions ouvrières, 1993).

answered with the sung acclamation "Thanks be to God." What is our reaction to this? After seeing the flame, after hearing the proclamation, how do we engage with this dramatic symbol? Clearly most people, if asked, would say this symbol has to do celebrating with the Resurrection of Christ—his triumph over sin and death that is celebrated in a special way at the Easter vigil. This would be the corporate meaning. But a symbol is heuristic—it triggers a variety of associations that come to mind, depending upon our own history and what is happening in our lives. To a wife who has just lost her husband after forty years of happy marriage, the paschal candle can evoke hope in the resurrection of the dead, linked with grateful memories and prayers for her husband. To a young person wrestling with emotional problems, it could be a reassuring affirmation of Christ's presence in what is experienced as a time of frustration and loneliness. It is because the symbol can both convey and elicit personal and corporate meaning at the same time that the response "Thanks be to God" can be simultaneously a corporate and personal affirmation of faith linked to the life situation of every believer. This multivalent nature of symbol both unites us with others and enables us to promote an involvement, an active participation in the liturgy that would be impossible by other means.

## MYSTAGOGY AND PARTICIPATION

In order to help this symbolic language of our liturgy speak and engender active participation—especially in our technological age, which tends to dull our perception of symbolic communication—there is an increasing interest in returning to an ancient form of catechesis known as mystagogy in order to recapture the power of ritual and symbol. Pope Benedict XVI noted in *Sacramentum caritatis* that there is a need to help the faithful "make their interior dispositions correspond to their gestures and words."[53] Along with the participants at the 2005 Synod on the Eucharist, he suggests that the best approach to formation of this type is mystagogy, or using experience of the symbols and signs of the liturgy itself as the point of departure for catechesis and reflection on the faith. Here an intrinsic link can be made between the *ars celebrandi* and active participation.

In order for this approach to be effective we must take another look at our liturgical practice—the way we celebrate the rites. We

---

53  SacCar, no. 64.

need to go beyond rationalism and minimalism, common in some quarters of the Church in the United States, in our use of liturgical and sacramental symbols. This attitude tends to focus only on the minimum necessary for the valid conferral of the sacrament without paying much attention to the liturgy's "signs perceptible to the senses." This also leads to the issue of the connection between what we say and what we do in our celebrations. The practice of the "liturgical lie"—saying or doing something in the liturgy that is patently untrue—is still a big problem. What Christopher Walsh trenchantly observed almost thirty years ago about Britain is equally true today of the United States:

> To my mind the principal problem, indeed crisis, facing liturgy in this country is that of credibility. Despite all the revision and reform (and sometimes perhaps because of it), a hiatus amounting in many cases to a chasm of Grand Canyon proportions has opened up between language and experience, between description and reality, between ideology and fact. Thus "families" whose members know nothing of each other, "communities" which are nothing of the sort, "songs" which are recited, "acclamations" which are muttered by one voice, baptisms where people are "bathed" and "buried" with Christ under 10 ml of water and "welcomed into a community" which has not bothered to turn up and even been informed of the event, "meals" at which no one drinks and where "sharing one bread" means simultaneous consumption of 500 individual breads, "gifts of the people" which are the joyless and perfunctory discharge of an obligation. The list is depressing and almost infinitely extensible.[54]

If we are to turn to the mystagogical approach to catechesis, it is imperative that we work at the quality of our celebrations. It is in the liturgy that Catholics experience the faith and come into contact with the traditions of the Church. This was known in the first millennium as "first theology" (*theologia prima*). Liturgical scholars such as Alexander Schmemann and Aidan Kavanagh insist that the experience of liturgical worship is "the ontological condition of theology" and the *sine qua non* of coming to any adequate appreciation of the faith

---

54 Christopher J. Walsh, "Task Unfinished," in *English Catholic Worship: Liturgical Renewal in England Since 1900*, eds. J. D. Crichton, H. E. Winstone, and J. R. Ainslie (London: Geoffrey Chapman, 1979), 139-140.

of the Church.[55] It is for this reason that the integrity of the liturgical celebration itself is so important both for participation and for mystagogy. Kathleen Hughes points out the crucial necessity of good liturgy in *Saying Amen: A Mystagogy of Sacrament*:

> The most critical element for successful mystagogy is well-celebrated rites. Excellent, care-full, well-planned and well-executed liturgy is first-level mystagogy. . . . the liturgy is first theology, that is, . . . liturgy is the most immediate, most condensed statement of who we are and what we believe. Good liturgy is an absolute prerequisite to rich symbol participation and contemplation. The strong warning of the American bishops must be heeded in this regard: Good liturgy nourishes faith; poor liturgy destroys it.[56]

Clearly, attending to the quality of our liturgical celebrations is crucial if we are to expect that the baptized will be able to enter into them "fully, consciously, and actively." In light of fostering active participation, let us turn now to particular symbolic languages in which the liturgy speaks.

## GESTURES, MOVEMENT, POSTURE

One of the key ways that we can promote full, conscious, and active participation is to encourage "mindfulness"[57] regarding one of the basic languages of the liturgy: gestures, movements, and posture. These are not the monopoly of the priest celebrant or other ministers; they belong to every member of the assembly. We often take for granted the bodily gestures we perform in the liturgy, having practiced them all our lives; but attending to this basic part of our involvement in the rite is a good place to begin any mystagogical

---

55  See Alexander Schmemann, *Introduction to Liturgical Theology* (London: The Faith Press, 1966), and Aidan Kavanagh, *On Liturgical Theology* (New York: Pueblo, 1984).

56  Kathleen Hughes, *Saying Amen: A Mystagogy of Sacrament* (Chicago: Liturgy Training Publications, 1999), 16. The last statement in the quotation is an echo of the 1972 USCCB document *Music in Catholic Worship* (rev. ed. [Washington, DC: USCCB, 1982]), no. 6: "Faith grows when it is well expressed in celebration. Good celebrations foster and nourish faith. Poor celebrations weaken and destroy faith." Due to its importance, this statement has been repeated in the latest USCCB document on liturgical music, *Sing to the Lord: Music in Divine Worship* (STL) (Washington, DC: USCCB, 2007), no. 5.

57  On mindfulness, contemplation, and paying attention, see Hughes, "Paying Attention," in *Saying Amen*, 17-32.

catechesis. These gestures, along with the other "languages" of the liturgy, call us to corporate worship:

> Because of the indissoluble unity of the human person as "body/soul," corporeal gestures are capable of bearing transcendent significance. Bodily gestures are thus not merely educative or instrumental; they are "doors to the transcendent" that actually open us to the presence and impact of Mystery. Bodily gestures do not merely "describe an attitude"; *they enact the relationship described by that attitude.* Dropping to one's knees enacts adoration, supplication, contrition or repentance—it does not simply "describe" these things or "educate" us in their desirability or significance.[58]

This is one of the elements alluded to by Romano Guardini when he spoke of "relearning forgotten ways of doing things" during the implementation of the reforms of Vatican II. An example of one of these "forgotten ways" is well described in his meditation on making the sign of the Cross.

> When we cross ourselves, let it be with a real sign of the cross. Instead of a small cramped gesture that gives no notion of its meaning, let us make a large unhurried sign from forehead to breast, from shoulder to shoulder, consciously feeling how it includes the whole of us—our thoughts, our attitudes, our body and soul, every part of us at once—how it consecrates and sanctifies us. . . . It does so because it is the sign of the universe and the signs of our redemption. On the cross Christ redeemed [hu]mankind. By the cross he sanctifies us to the last shred and fiber of our being. We make the sign of the cross before we pray to collect and compose ourselves and to fix our minds and hearts and wills upon God. We make it when we finish praying in order that we may hold fast the gift we have received from God.[59]

---

58   John K. Leonard and Nathan D. Mitchell, *Postures of the Assembly During the Eucharistic Prayer* (Chicago: Liturgy Training Publications, 1994), 16.

59   Romano Guardini, *Sacred Signs* (St. Louis: Pio Decimo Press, 1956), 13, cited in Gabe Huck and Gerald T. Chinchar, *Liturgy with Style and Grace* (Chicago: Liturgy Training Publications, 1998), 21.

The GIRM speaks of the gestures and postures of the ministers and the people. These gestures "ought to contribute to making the entire celebration resplendent with beauty and noble simplicity, so that the true and full meaning of the different parts of the celebration is evident and that the participation of all is fostered."[60] It should be noted, however, that catechesis will need to be provided—especially in multicultural assemblies—regarding the gesture and posture of the assembly at the Eucharist, because there are important variations from culture to culture and from nation to nation with regard to when to kneel during the Eucharistic Prayer, whether to use the "*orans*" posture for the Our Father that is commonly assumed by all members of the assembly in certain places, and even whether the assembly stands or sits for the reading of the Gospel. As *Varietates legitimae* states:

> The gestures and postures of the assembly are signs of its unity and express its active participation and foster the spiritual attitude of the participants. Each culture will choose those gestures and bodily postures which express the attitude of humanity before God, giving them a Christian significance, having some relationship if possible, with the gestures and postures of the Bible.[61]

## ARCHITECTURE AND ENVIRONMENT

Architecture has an undeniable role in promoting active participation. The USCCB document on art, architecture, and worship, *Built of Living Stones*—referencing both the *Code of Canon Law* and *Sacrosanctum Concilium*—says it well:

> *The church building fosters participation in the liturgy.* Because liturgical actions by their nature are communal celebrations, they are celebrated with the presence and active participation of the Christian faithful whenever possible. Such participation, both internal and external, is the faithful's "right and duty by reason of their baptism." The building itself can promote or hinder the "full conscious and active participation" of the faithful. Parishes making decisions about

---

60   GIRM, no. 42.

61   VL, no. 41.

the design of a church must consider how the various aspects and choices they make will affect the ability of all the members to participate fully in liturgical celebrations.[62]

While *Built of Living Stones* is mindful that church buildings need to be sensitive to the cultural diversity of Catholics in the United States and that there is a need for ongoing inculturation,[63] this document rightly emphasizes that the liturgical space needs to allow for the physical, visible, and public expressions that make up the liturgy and are necessary for active participation of the assembly in the rites. It also notes that "today the Church in the United States is again exploring how to translate the Gospel and to build churches in conversation with complex, secularized cultures that have sometimes rejected religion and attempted their own forms of human transcendence through intricate electronic modes of communication, art, and architecture."[64] Importantly, though, the document also leaves the door open to creativity in speaking about art and architecture, affirming that "the Church is not exclusively identified with the forms of the past."[65]

One of the issues about church construction and design affecting active participation that was not raised in *Built of Living Stones* has to do with the size of churches being built in the United States. The larger the church, the more difficult participation becomes. As the number of priests diminishes, there is a temptation in many dioceses to build larger and larger churches. The problems that distance from the liturgical action poses for active participation need to be taken seriously. Unlike the mega-church movement that engages crowds in an auditorium-like space through the use of projection screens, Catholic liturgy requires a smaller scale in order to be truly participatory. As noted liturgical designer Fr. Richard Vosko has pointed out:

If "full, active and conscious participation" during the liturgy of the Eucharist, which "is not a private act," is a standard principle, and if we do not wish to betray our primary symbols system during worship by resorting to big screen

---

62  USCCB, *Built of Living Stones: Art, Architecture, and Worship: Guidelines of the United States Conference of Catholic Bishops* (BLS) (Washington, DC: USCCB, 2000), no. 31.

63  See BLS, nos. 6, 38, 41, 42, and 43.

64  BLS, no. 42.

65  BLS, no. 45.

projections, then studies in the behavioral sciences and building design must be heeded when creating churches that are to engage worshipers in the rituals and not render them passive spectators.[66]

The use of the plastic arts in worship—painting, sculpture, textiles—are all potential media for promoting participation. *Built of Living Stones*, paragraph 155, makes a helpful distinction between liturgical and devotional art and the need for both in the parish. In practice, though, this distinction may sometimes be a bit unclear. Since many cultural groups identify strongly with certain sacred images—the Mexican community with Our Lady of Guadalupe, for example—it is often unthinkable for a given cultural group within a parish not to have that sacred image visible in the main body of the church, as opposed to a devotional area out of the sight of the assembly. Obviously, dialogue with the community is important, but the distinction between art that serves the liturgical action and art that is primarily private and devotional needs to inform the placement and use of art in the liturgical space.

## Music

We have seen that documents on sacred music by Pope Pius X and Pope Pius XI at the beginning of the twentieth century were the first to voice the phrase "active participation" and affirm its necessity among the faithful in the liturgy. Of all the various ways in which the faithful are called to participate in the liturgy, music is clearly one of the most important. The recent USCCB statement on liturgical music, *Sing to the Lord*, underlines the crucial role played by musical participation in worship. This document links liturgy to Christian witness through a paraphrase of one the best-known passages of Vatican II's Pastoral Constitution on the Church in the Modern World, Gaudium et spes: "Christ, whose praises we have sung, remains with us and leads us through church doors to the whole world, with its joys and hopes, griefs and anxieties."[67] Works of love, justice, and evangelization are also inspired and strengthened by such participation. "Charity, justice, and evangelization are thus the

---

66  Richard S. Vosko, "Built of Living Stones: Seven Years Later," *Liturgical Ministry* 17 (Spring 2008): 88.

67  STL, no. 8.

normal consequences of liturgical celebration. Particularly inspired by sung participation, the body of the Word Incarnate goes forth to spread the Gospel with full force and compassion."[68] Although in some areas we have been slow to appreciate it, the assembly's sung participation in worship is regarded by the liturgical reform not just as a nice extra but as an intrinsic part of the liturgy.[69]

*Sing to the Lord* also discusses both internal and external participation, indicating that at times our participation may be internal, when we listen to prayers voiced by the priest celebrant or music sung by the choir.[70] At other times "participation must also be external, so that internal participation can be expressed and reinforced by actions, gestures, and bodily attitudes, and by the acclamations, responses, and singing."[71]

Musical participation, as important as it is, often becomes problematic due to a variety of factors—many of which are cultural. Attending to the musical differences engendered by culture is crucial if we are going to promote real musical participation of the assembly—especially in multicultural parishes. Musicologist Linda O'Brien-Rohe has pointed out that we need to go beyond the romantic notion that music is "a universal language" and that it is capable of communicating the same thing to people of a variety of cultures at the same time. The interpretations given to tempo, key, and musical form vary a great deal from culture to culture and need to be taken into account when one composes and proposes music for the assembly.[72] It is for this reason that *Sing to the Lord*, referencing the GIRM, emphasizes that "liturgical music must always be chosen and sung 'with due consideration for the culture of the people and abilities of each liturgical assembly.'"[73]

*Sing to the Lord* moves forward the conversation on music in our assemblies by proposing a goal of musical interculturality. While we are mindful of the need to respect the integrity of cultural expressions of the faith in the liturgy, in multicultural parishes real participation in the life of the parish invites us all to allow our

---

68   STL, no. 9.

69   Participation of the assembly is the basic thrust of this document. See the excellent commentary by Anthony Ruff, "Sing to the Lord: Music in Divine Worship," *Liturgical Ministry* 17 (Spring 2008): 77-84.

70   See STL, no. 12.

71   STL, no. 13.

72   See Linda O'Brien-Rohe, "Music in the Multicultural Parish," *Liturgical Life* (May-June 1993).

73   STL, no. 58, referencing GIRM, no. 40.

particular cultural expressions to be enriched by the people of the other cultures with whom we share the parish:

> When prepared with an attitude of mutual reciprocity, local communities might eventually expand from those celebrations that merely highlight their multicultural differences to celebrations that better reflect the intercultural relationships of the assembly and the unity that is shared in Christ. Likewise, the valuable musical gifts of the diverse cultural and ethnic communities should enrich the whole Church in the United States by contributing to the repertory of liturgical song and to the growing richness of Christian faith.[74]

*Sing to the Lord* also encourages the use of Latin in multicultural and international liturgical gatherings and calls for the development of a parish repertoire of Gregorian chant. At the same time, the document is also pastorally realistic. Since not every cultural group has the same cultural relation to the Latin language, the document ends its section on Latin with this caveat: "Whenever the Latin language poses an obstacle to singers, even after sufficient training has been provided—for example, in pronunciation, understanding of the text, or confident rendition of a piece—it would be more prudent to employ a vernacular language in the Liturgy."[75]

Clearly, the value of active musical participation of the assembly, without excluding the musical ministry of a choir or other soloists, is at the heart of this document from the USCCB. *Sing to the Lord*'s development of the principle of "progressive solemnity"[76] helps place sacred music squarely in the service of the liturgical assembly. All of this means that the choice of music, linked to an appropriate judgment as to the parts of the Mass that ought to be sung, should eschew ostentation or empty ceremonialism in light of the role of the assembly.[77]

---

74   STL, no. 59.

75   STL, no. 64. On the use of Latin in culturally diverse communities, see my article "The 'Supra-Regional Roman' Rite: An Answer for our Multicultural Assemblies?", *Pastoral Music* 27:4 (April, May 2003): 62-64.

76   STL, no. 110; see STL, nos. 110-114.

77   STL, footnote 87, references *Musicam Sacram*, no. 11: "It should be borne in mind that the true solemnity of liturgical worship depends less on a more ornate form of singing and a more magnificent ceremonial than on its worthy and religious celebration, which takes into account the integrity of the liturgical celebration itself, and the performance of each of its parts according to their own particular nature."

# CONCLUSION: LITURGY, LIFE, AND CONVERSION

As we strive to promote full, conscious, and active participation, it is essential that we not lose sight of the extra-liturgical connection that makes this participation authentic. At heart, it is a question of liturgy and life. A prerequisite for the authenticity of lay liturgical participation is the legitimate participation of all of the baptized in the life of the Church. We will inadvertently promote a "liturgical lie" if we work for lay participation in the liturgy but then deny lay participation outside of the liturgy due to an inappropriate clericalism. The late Mark Searle stated it well:

> It has become increasingly clear that active participation in the liturgy on the basis of baptism is something of a sham if it does not mean active participation in the whole life of the local church and the assuming of wider responsibilities of the Church toward its members and the larger society which flow from the liturgy being merely the source and summit of Christian life. The faithful will not be able to make the desired connection between liturgy and daily life if their participation in the life of the believing community is restricted to liturgical role playing.[78]

As we introduce the new translation of the *Missale Romanum*, it is important that we keep the reason for the Council's original goal of active participation clear in our minds. Understanding active participation in light of the liturgical movement, and inspired by Pope Pius X's affirmation that active participation in the liturgy is the primary and indispensable source from which the faithful derive the true Christian spirit, the Council announced an overarching desire "to impart an ever increasing vigor to the Christian life of the faithful."[79] We are not starting from scratch. The fruits of the Council's call for the laity's "full, conscious and active participation in the liturgy" have already been realized in most parishes in the United States. These fruits need to be built upon. We have learned over the years that the real goal is what liturgical theologian Mary Collins

---

78 Mark Searle, "Reflections on Liturgical Reform," in *Vision: The Scholarly Contributions of Mark Searle to Liturgical Renewal*, ed. Anne Y. Koester and Barbara Searle (Collegeville, MN: The Liturgical Press, 2004), 90.

79 SC, no. 1 (DOL 1).

has called "contemplative participation."[80] This can be described as being mindful of how and why we participate in the liturgy so that we allow ourselves to be transformed by God's grace into the Body of Christ for the life of the world.

The goal of active liturgical participation is not mindless activism. It is all about conversion: how we see in Christ's Passion, Death, and Resurrection the pattern and promise for our own lives—that we might live no longer for ourselves, but for Christ (see 2 Cor 5:15). This goal was clear in the minds of the pioneers of the liturgical movement, and we lose sight of it at our peril. Years before Pius XII's *Mystici Corporis*, during the height of the Depression, Catherine de Hueck Doherty—one of the great lay voices for social justice—expressed it so well:

> The daily sacrifice, fully participated in, will open to us the mind of Christ, and we will radiate him in our lives. And then we shall be able to go forth and fight the good fight of Christ against poverty, misery, injustice. Participation in the Mass will teach us the full understanding of the Mystical Body of Christ, leading us to a Christian sociology which is the cornerstone of the Christian social order and which alone can save our mad world from destruction.[81]

Almost fifty years after *Sacrosanctum Concilium*, this goal is what is still at stake in the liturgical participation of God's people.

---

80  Mary Collins, *Contemplative Participation:* Sacrosanctum Concilium *Twenty-Five Years Later* (Collegeville, MN: The Liturgical Press, 1990), 83.

81  Catherine de Hueck Doherty, "I Saw Christ Today," *Orate Fratres* 12 (1938): 309-310. Cited in Gilbert Ostdiek's excellent essay, "Liturgy and Justice: The Legacy That Awaits Us," in *Liturgy and Justice: To Worship God in Spirit and Truth*, ed. Anne Y. Koester (Collegeville, MN: The Liturgical Press, 2002), 6.

# CHAPTER 4

# Divining the Vernacular of Ritual Texts

Rev. Paul Turner

The translation of Latin liturgical texts into myriad vernacular languages for the purpose of worship is a relatively recent enterprise in the Roman Catholic Church and a task for which there is no clear historical parallel in any century or within any other corporate entity. In the first several centuries of Christianity, believers prayed in their vernacular languages, but usually not in translation. Ministers and writers crafted or improvised prayers and songs in the language of the gathered assembly. Some sharing between language groups took place, especially between Greek and Latin, but the exchange was comparatively limited. By the sixth century a corpus of Latin prayers, hymns, and rubrics coalesced in collections of ordos and sacramentaries, antiphonaries and pontificals. Ministers, who had a working knowledge of Latin, used these widely. At the same time, however, modern languages were evolving on the streets, and Latin, which gained strength as the language for worship in the churches of the Roman Rite, was losing its foothold as a vernacular language. The rise of modern languages became more established by the eleventh century. Through all this time, Latin endured as a language for worship. Translations into the growing number of vernacular languages did not seem important for purposes of liturgical prayer.

The Church was not alone in its esteem for Latin. In Western civilization, Latin remained the preferred language for scholarship and politics, for philosophy, science, and the arts. Facility with the language was necessary to understand history through the eyes of figures such as Caesar and Cicero. The study of Latin remained important through and beyond the Renaissance. Michelangelo, who died in 1564, did not know much Latin; but Galileo, born that same year, did, and he used it extensively to communicate his discoveries and opinions to a wide audience. To this day, many treatises written during this period have never been translated into modern languages, so an appreciation of the history of Western civilization still requires a facility with Latin.

In the twentieth century, in the interests of enhancing the participation of the entire assembly at worship, the Catholic Church authorized the use of the vernacular for its liturgy, by way of translation. The results have been overwhelmingly positive. The vernacular has allowed the faithful to pray with greater understanding, to find deeper spiritual connections between the Tradition of the Church and their daily lives, and to formulate a voice and style of worship that fits the challenges and blessings of their day. It took courage to change centuries of liturgical tradition, but the Fathers of the Second Vatican Council achieved it with much prayer under the pastoral guidance of Popes John XXIII and Paul VI. To be sure, some within the Church—and outside it—have lamented the loss of Latin from the liturgy. But the experience of Sunday worshipers in parish churches around the world has shown that the decision in favor of the vernacular was truly a gift of the Holy Spirit. This is not the first generation to use a vernacular language for worship in the Roman Rite, but it is the first to incorporate and use translations on a wide scale.

The process of translation, therefore, has come under great scrutiny in the past few decades, and the principles governing that process have shifted, based on experience with modern languages and deeper reflection on Tradition. Catholics have become very comfortable praying in the vernacular, and one sign that the venture has succeeded is that many worshipers do not consciously realize that the words they use are translations. The words have suited their needs, but scholars and linguists familiar with the originals and with modern modes of expression have obtained a growing awareness that the translations could be improved. The Church is still feeling its way through this dark linguistic forest. Which theory of translation best suits the needs of the traditional texts and of the people who pray them? How uniform should vernacular translations be between the various modern languages? Who should hold the authority for writing and approving vernacular translations? What place would new regional compositions hold in the complete body of the Church's euchology? What range of vocabulary is appropriate for worship? What linguistic register best fits the experience of worship? Questions such as these have opened up a healthy if at times painful debate over the sound of Catholic worship.

This situation has no clear historical parallel. Outside the Catholic Church, other entities face the need for accurate translations. Multinational corporations have to communicate in multiple languages, and a consumer may have to choose from half a dozen languages when reading the instructions for the proper use of a newly purchased kitchen blender. But such information deals with modern texts composed in modern languages, and the number of languages—which may seem excessive to the average purchaser—pales before the number of liturgical languages for which vernacular translations of the Roman Rite must be made.

There are historical similarities to the challenge of translating great classical works such as *The Iliad*, but even the prayer over the gifts for the Fourteenth Sunday in Ordinary Time is heard in public more widely than a single verse of Homer. The best comparison is to the struggles surrounding biblical translations, a debate that has raged for millennia. How literal should the vernacular scriptures be? When does a paraphrase best help convey the meaning? In modern English, does the inclusion of archaisms such as "thee" and "thou" enhance the sacrality of the text? Debates about the meaning of the verses of the Bible inspired a more studied reflection on the theory of translation, which, it will be seen, in turn affected the rendering of vernacular liturgical texts in the Catholic Church after the Second Vatican Council.

In truth, the Latin original of the Catholic Church's prayers and rubrics is not always as ancient as it seems. Many prayers based on sources from antiquity have been re-edited for the sake of theological precision or linguistic grace. Some texts were newly composed in Latin after the Second Vatican Council—and often their quality does not measure up to the prayers that are centuries old.

For example, one of the original third- to fourth-century sources for Eucharistic Prayer II includes this phrase about Jesus: "who, when he was conceived [and] made flesh, was shown to be your Son, being born of the Holy Spirit and the Virgin."[1] But this could be understood to mean that Jesus was not the Son of God before he was born. When this prayer was added to the *Missal* in 1969, it was trimmed for the sake of theological precision. The forthcoming translation states it this way: "incarnate by the Holy Spirit and born

---

1     Quoted in Paul F. Bradshaw, Maxwell E. Johnson, and L. Edward Philipps, *The Apostolic Tradition: A Commentary* (Minneapolis: Augsburg Fortress Press, 2002), 39.

of the Virgin."[2] No mention is made of how in the Incarnation Jesus "was shown to be" God's Son.

An example of a newly composed prayer for the *Missal* is the collect for the votive Mass of Our Lady, Mother of the Church. The Mass was added as an expression of the Mariology stemming from the Second Vatican Council. A literal (though not usable) English rendering of the Latin prayer might run something like this: "O God, the Father of mercies, whose Only-Begotten Sun hung upon the Cross, chose the Blessed Virgin Mary, his Mother, to be our Mother also, grant, we pray, that with her loving help your Church may be every day more fruitful, exult in the holiness of her children, and draw to her embrace all families of peoples." The final translation of this prayer will probably be less complex, but even a casual observer can note that the prayer's author desired to include a wide variety of images in a single, multilayered sentence that reads better on paper than it can be proclaimed in public. The problems with this prayer stem from its composition, not merely from its translation. The prayer exists in the *Missal*, so it has to be translated as part of the project, and the work must observe the current rules for translation. The result will show the good intentions but minimal skills of the more recent author when compared with some of the prayers from antiquity.

In any case, the entire enterprise is new—translating from an ancient language for modern usage in an extraordinarily diverse range of languages. Some complaints about the results are justified, but on the whole, the Church has been performing this task remarkably well. The translations currently in use have helped a generation of Catholics use their own language in liturgical prayer. Now, after several decades of experience, the Church is ready to try again to achieve even better results.

Translation is an art. There are usually many ways to say something. ("I'd like a glass of milk." "Would you please give me a glass of milk?" "Bring me some milk." "Gimme milk, please.") The artistry lies in finding the way that says it best according to circumstances—to divine the right translation. People who know only one language may find this concept difficult to grasp. Many of them assume there is a one-to-one correspondence between words in one language and their mates in another. But a simple glance at any dictionary shows the multiple definitions that exist for any one word within

2    "Parts of the Order of Mass," *www.usccb.org/liturgy/missalformation/OrdoMissaeWhiteBook.pdf*, accessed August 24, 2008.

one language. Words strung together into a phrase or sentence may create a new meaning beyond their individual parts. The setting, the person being addressed, and the occasion all may alter the vocabulary people choose to make their point. Everyone has had the sorry experience of saying the wrong word when a better choice would have saved face—or a relationship.

In setting about its vernacular translations, the Catholic Church faces several challenges: how to be faithful to the historicity of the texts, choose the right words and phrases, find a text that can be proclaimed—not just read—effectively, and let the words do what they were intended to do—help believers pray.

# THE EVOLUTION OF
# THE *ROMAN MISSAL*

"SACRAMENTARY" is the word that adorns the binding of a book that English-speaking worshipers have seen a server hold and a priest consult for the prayers they hear at Mass. It is the English translation of a book that bears the Latin title *Missale Romanum*. Prior to the Second Vatican Council, the *Missale Romanum* contained the readings and prayers of the Mass bound together in the same volume; the Council separated the readings into a different publication, the Lectionary. In English the remaining volume became known as the Sacramentary because it now had the content of books that bore that title from the sixth to the fifteenth century. However, the Latin title never changed. Consequently, English-speaking Catholics today are used to calling the *Missale Romanum* their Sacramentary.

The first book bearing the title *Missale Romanum* appeared in 1474. Prior to that time there existed ordos, sacramentaries, antiphonals, and pontificals, and some of these were combined, amplified, and ameliorated. But the first book calling itself a "Roman Missal" appeared before the Reformation and before the Council of Trent. That Council steered a number of reforms throughout the Catholic world, and among these was the reform of the *Missal*, which was then published in 1570. "The Missal of 1570 differs very little from the very first printed edition of 1474, which in turn faithfully follows the Missal used at the time of Pope Innocent III [+1216]."[3]

---

3 *General Instruction of the Roman Missal* (GIRM) (Washington, DC: United States Conference of Catholic Bishops [USCCB], 2003), no. 7.

Trent's *Missal* underwent some minor revisions over the centuries, but it maintained its basic structure and content for four hundred years. Its first major revision resulted from the work of the Second Vatican Council in the 1960s. The *General Instruction of the Roman Missal* (GIRM) explains that the revised *Missal* is a natural evolution of its predecessors: "the liturgical norms of the Council of Trent have certainly been completed and perfected in many respects by those of the Second Vatican Council, which has brought to realization the efforts of the last four hundred years to bring the faithful closer to the Sacred Liturgy."[4]

If you ask the average Catholic to name the two most significant liturgical reforms of the Second Vatican Council, you will probably hear something like this: "The priest says Mass facing the people. The Mass is in the vernacular." The second response is hard to argue, but the first is only part of the story. The revised *Missal* introduced significant changes to the content of the Mass while retaining its basic traditional form. Prior to the Council, the altar was fixed against the back wall of the church. The priest led the prayers from there, reading from the *Missal*. He turned to the people for the greetings and some other parts of the service, but the look of a Mass in process was the view of the back of the priest. The introduction of the freestanding altar was a significant feature of the revised Order of Mass,[5] but quite a number of additional changes were made to the texts and rituals of the Mass: the removal of many repetitions, the elimination of the prayers at the foot of the altar, the simplification of the concluding rites, the insertion of the prayer of the faithful, and the adding of memorial acclamations, to name a few. Many Catholics found these changes to be of little consequence because they were experiencing Mass in the vernacular for the first time. The most obvious ritual change to them was the relocation of the altar from the back wall to the center of the sanctuary, with the consequent reorientation of the priest.

The revision of the rites was the first significant liturgical reform of the Council. The second, the introduction of the vernacular, allowed people to participate at Mass with greater understanding. Although these two liturgical reforms were distinct, they are often conflated in the minds of the public, many of whom refer to the Mass before Vatican II as "the Latin Mass"—even though the post-

---

4    GIRM, no. 15.

5    See GIRM, no. 299.

conciliar Mass is itself a Latin Mass, and the distinction between the preconciliar and postconciliar Masses is more one of content, style, and participation.

# THE *ROMAN MISSAL* OF THE SECOND VATICAN COUNCIL

The *Roman Missal* of the Second Vatican Council has continued to evolve. Even before the Council concluded its work, the Sacred Congregation of Rites promulgated on January 25, 1965, an Order of Mass—the words and rubrics to be used for every Mass every day. This would need further revision, but it introduced the vernacular for the people's parts, while keeping the private prayers of the priest and the entire Roman Canon in Latin.[6] This Order of Mass introduced some simplifications to the preconciliar Mass, but it still retained the prayers at the foot of the altar and observed the former calendar. When this order was made available in English the following year, congregations sang "Holy, Holy, Holy, Lord God of hosts," and answered the greeting "The Lord be with you" with the words "And with your spirit."

The group responsible for the translation was the newly formed International Commission on English in the Liturgy (ICEL). It was founded as a mixed commission—that is, a commission drawing members from a variety of episcopal conferences sharing the same language. In the case of English, the conferences were those of Australia, Canada, England and Wales, India, Ireland, New Zealand, Pakistan, the Philippines, Scotland, South Africa, and the United States. A permanent secretariat was staffed in Washington, D.C., to carry out the commission's work.

The revised Order of Mass, which replaced the 1965 interim rite, was published in Latin in 1969. Work on the vernacular translation began immediately. In fact, the English translation of the new Order of Mass was published the following year.[7] Even though parts of the Mass were being prayed in English for a few years, the Order of Mass was not settled until 1970. The translation of the rest of the *Missal* was not yet ready, but the use of this much of it could begin.

---

6   See *The English-Latin Sacramentary for the United States of America: The Prayers of the Celebrant of Mass Together with the Ordinary of the Mass* (New York: Catholic Book Publishing Co., 1966).

7   See *The Order of Mass* (New York: Catholic Book Publishing Co., 1970).

This translation is the one that English-speaking congregations have used ever since: "And also with you," "Holy, Holy, Holy Lord, God of power and might," and so on.

It took four years to translate, approve, and publish the full Sacramentary in English, which appeared in 1974. The name of the book in Latin remained *Missale Romanum*, but the English translation was now called the Sacramentary.[8]

Rome promulgated a second Latin edition of the *Missale Romanum* in 1975 to update the text with other developments in the liturgy. For example, the office of subdeacon had been suppressed in 1973, and the rubrics concerning that minister needed to be reassigned to acolytes and readers. Entrance and communion antiphons were added to some Mass formulas for various needs and occasions. Some other Mass formulas were inserted, including the Dedication of a Church and an Altar; Mary, the Mother of the Church; and the Most Holy Name of Mary. Eucharistic prayers for Masses with Children and for Masses of Reconciliation were also included. Other appendices were added. Some headings and rubrics were changed to correspond to other liturgical books that had been published in the interim.

The second edition of the *Missal* appeared in English in 1985, and it is the Sacramentary in use in Catholic parishes today.[9] There was virtually no change to the parts that had already been translated in the previous edition. Those parts that had been added to the second edition in Latin were translated, approved, and included.

Shortly after this, ICEL decided to work again on the entire Sacramentary. The texts had been in use for several decades, and their strengths and shortcomings were becoming more evident. Over the years, ICEL had been gaining experience in the free composition of new texts, as it was becoming more skilled at rendering translations in a maturing vernacular voice.

Examples of ICEL's revisions can be found in the 1989 Order of Christian Funerals. One of the prayers for general circumstances in the funeral rite of 1969 had carried this translation: "Lord, hear our prayers and be merciful to your son (daughter) N., whom you have called from this life. Welcome him (her) into the company of your saints, in the kingdom of light and peace."[10] Twenty years later the

---

8    See *The Sacramentary* (New York: Catholic Book Publishing Co., 1974).

9    See *The Sacramentary* (New York: Catholic Book Publishing Co., 1985).

10    *Rite of Funerals*, no. 33, in the 1976 edition of *The Rites* (New York: Pueblo, 1976), 645.

revised translation of the same prayer said it this way: "Lord, in our grief we turn to you. Are you not the God of love who opens your ears to all? Listen to our prayers for your servant N., whom you have called out of this world: lead him/her to your kingdom of light and peace and count him/her among the saints in glory."[11] The revised funeral liturgy also included this newly composed prayer for the death of a young person: "Lord God, source and destiny of our lives, in your loving providence you gave us N. to grow in wisdom, age, and grace. Now you have called him/her to yourself. As we grieve the loss of one so young, we seek to understand your purpose. Draw him/her to yourself and give him/her full stature in Christ. May he/she stand with all the angels and saints who know your love and praise your saving will."[12] The style of translation and the composition of new texts fit within the responsibilities that ICEL had undertaken from its foundation. Its work was approved by the then National Conference of Catholic Bishops in the United States and by the Congregation for Divine Worship in Rome.

The retranslation of the second edition of the Sacramentary began in 1983, and the first pieces emerged in 1992. The work was prepared in eight parts and was submitted to ICEL's eleven English-speaking conferences of bishops around the world. Gradually, the new translation was approved by all of them, and it was sent in 1998 to the Congregation for Divine Worship and the Discipline of the Sacraments for approval.[13]

Approval never came. Instead, the Congregation, which had been concerned about the style of translation in texts for the liturgy, issued new directives governing the principles of translation. The resulting instruction, *Liturgiam authenticam* (2001), hailed by supporters and denounced by detractors,[14] became the law of the Church and reset the stage for translation. Among its decisions was the elimination of the composition of original texts from the responsibilities of mixed commissions such as ICEL.[15]

---

11   *Order of Christian Funerals* (OCF), no. 398:2, in the 1990 edition of *The Rites* (New York: Pueblo, 1990), 909.

12   OCF, no. 398:28.

13   See John Wilkins, "Lost in Translation: The Bishops, the Vatican and the English Liturgy," *Commonweal*, December 2, 2005.

14   See, for example, Peter Jeffrey, "A Chant Historian Reads *Liturgiam authenticam*," *Worship* 78:1 (January 2004), 78:2 (March 2004), 78:3 (May 2004), and 78:4 (July 2004).

15   Congregation for Divine Worship and the Discipline of the Sacraments, *Liturgiam authenticam: Fifth Instruction on Vernacular Translation of the Roman Liturgy* (Washington, DC: USCCB, 2001), no. 98.

In the meantime, Pope John Paul II had promulgated a *third* edition of the *Missal* in 2000, which was published in Latin in 2002, and it now needed to be translated into the vernacular languages. This third edition added modifications, the need for which had come to light through the publication of other liturgical books, pastoral experience, and the revised *Code of Canon Law*. The calendar was expanded to include additional observances, notably for groups of martyrs from different parts of the world. There were new Mass formulas for the Common of the Blessed Virgin Mary. The Masses for Various Needs and Occasions were lightly rearranged. Prayers over the people were added for each day of Lent. The Eucharistic Prayer for Masses for Various Needs and Occasions was included. Many small changes were introduced in the liturgies of Holy Week, and the GIRM was revised.

The differences in the Latin of the second and third editions are small; the prayers are essentially the same. But the theory of translation changed, and that will make the third English edition of the *Missal* very different from the second. So many words have changed that the editorial improvements to the *Missal* will be easily overlooked.

Shortly after the third edition of the *Missal* was published in Latin, an English translation of the GIRM was made available so that the changes to the rubrics could be put into place. This was important because the rubrics had become liturgical law, but the law was unknowable by those who did not have access to the Latin edition of the *Missal* or who could not read it if they did. The English edition of the GIRM appeared in 2002 as an interim translation, and a revised one will accompany the final vernacular publication of the entire *Missal*.

# TRANSLATION ISSUES

The theory, process, and authority for liturgical translation have all changed since the Second Vatican Council. These changes fed suspicions that the Vatican was displeased with the state of translations in general and with the work of ICEL in particular. One significant problem was that, globally speaking, Latin is not known as well as English. Consequently, some vernacular translations around the world were being made from the English as a source text, not from the Latin.[16] As with any translation of a translation, the resulting texts

---

16    See *Liturgiam authenticam*, no. 24.

strayed further from the originals. Hence, it was becoming important that the English text adhere more closely to the Latin, so that those in other language groups who were using it to help make their own translations would find a closer link to the original source.

## THEORY

The instruction that initially governed the theory of translation is known by its French title, *Comme le prévoit*.[17] It was issued from Rome in 1969 by the Consilium responsible for implementing the liturgical reforms of Vatican II. This instruction says that a liturgical text "is a medium of spoken communication," whose purpose is "to proclaim the message of salvation to believers and to express the prayer of the Church to the Lord." It stated its theory of translation in broad strokes:

> To achieve this end, it is not sufficient that a liturgical trans-
> lation merely reproduce the expressions and ideas of the
> original text. Rather it must faithfully communicate to a
> given people, and in their own language, that which the
> Church by means of this given text originally intended to
> communicate to another people in another time. A faith-
> ful translation, therefore, cannot be judged on the basis of
> individual words: the total context of this specific act of
> communication must be kept in mind, as well as the literary
> form proper to the respective language.[18]

In liturgical circles, this theory has been called "dynamic equiv-
alence." Dynamic equivalence favors a translation of meanings, not necessarily a translation of individual words. The expression was borrowed from the work of Eugene Nida, who used it as a vehicle to advance a discussion on translations of the Bible. Nida explained dynamic equivalence as a form of translation to be evaluated by the successful reception of *meaning* in the receiver. Any translation, he argues, moves from a source to a receiver. The translator, who is first a receiver from the original source, becomes a source

---

17  See Consilium for Implementing the Constitution on the Sacred Liturgy, *Comme le prévoit*, in *The Liturgy Documents: A Parish Resource*, Vol. 2 (Chicago: Liturgy Training Publications, 1999), 235-242.

18  *Comme le prévoit*, no. 6.

for another receiver. The goal of translation is to make the original message understood by this new receiver:

> Dynamic equivalence is therefore to be defined in terms of the degree to which the receptors of the message in the receptor language respond to it in substantially the same manner as the receptors in the source language. This response can never be identical, for the cultural and historical settings are too different, but there should be a high degree of equivalence of response, or the translation will have failed to accomplish its purpose.[19]

This contrasts with what can be called "formal correspondence," which is sometimes called "formal equivalence." Nida explains:

> When we speak of verbal consistency in translating, we focus primary attention upon the way in which specific words are translated, but words are not the only formal feature involved in formal consistency. One may, for example, have formal consistency of word, phrase, and clause order (word order is, however, more difficult to retain than phrase or clause order), length of sentences, and classes for words, e.g., translating nouns by nouns and verbs by verbs. All of these formal features combine to produce what is called "formal correspondence," of which verbal consistency is merely one element.[20]

Dynamic equivalence is more than just getting across the basic meaning of an original source. It is more than a loose translation that sounds right because it captures the vocabulary and means of expression of the receiver language. It is rather a faithful communication of original meaning that may sacrifice some elements of a formal correspondence. For many years, ICEL's work was based on a theory of dynamic equivalence.

---

19    Eugene Albert Nida, *The Theory and Practice of Translation* (Leiden: E. J. Brill, 1969), 24.

20    Nida, *The Theory and Practice of Translation*, 22.

With the publication of *Liturgiam authenticam* in 2001, the Congregation for Divine Worship and the Discipline of the Sacraments (CDWDS) established new criteria for translation.

> The translation of the liturgical texts of the Roman Liturgy is not so much a work of creative innovation as it is of rendering the original texts faithfully and accurately into the vernacular language. While it is permissible to arrange the wording, the syntax and the style in such a way as to prepare a flowing vernacular text suitable to the rhythm of popular prayer, the original text, insofar as possible, must be translated integrally and in the most exact manner, without omissions or additions in terms of their content, and without paraphrases or glosses. Any adaptation to the characteristics or the nature of the various vernacular languages is to be sober and discreet.[21]

According to *Liturgiam authenticam*, capitalizations should copy those of the *editiones typicae* as much as possible.[22] The connections of clauses, word orders, and parallelisms are to be maintained,[23] and the texts should be usable for oral proclamation[24] and singing.[25] The CDWDS distributed further guidelines for translation in the *Ratio translationis*.[26] While *Liturgiam authenticam* gave general guidelines to be used in all vernacular translations, the *Ratio translationis* is a language-specific document, which makes—in this case—specific requests for translations into the English language.

The goal of all this was not to force a slavish word-for-word translation of the Latin, but rather to produce one that retains the content and structure of the Latin wherever possible, while honoring the demands for good oral proclamation of the texts, as well as their ease of comprehension.

---

21   *Liturgiam authenticam*, no. 20.

22   See *Liturgiam authenticam*, no. 33.

23   See *Liturgiam authenticam*, no. 57a.

24   See *Liturgiam authenticam*, no. 59.

25   See *Liturgiam authenticam*, no. 60.

26   See *Ratio translationis for the English Language* (Vatican City: Congregation for Divine Worship and the Discipline of the Sacraments, 2007).

## Process

In retrospect, one of the most remarkable elements of the postconciliar process of translation was the inclusion of representatives from other Christian bodies. Many of the texts that Roman Catholics use for worship today are also in use by other Christians at prayer. In an attempt to build upon the ecumenical movement, liturgists of different ecclesial bodies strove to achieve some common texts for worship, so that when a variety of Christians gathered as one, they might discover even in translation a potential source for deeper unity.

Since 1967 ICEL had engaged in dialogue with a representative group of several Christian communities, ultimately known as the Consultation on Common Texts. By the following year the meetings resulted in common texts for the Nicene Creed, the Apostles' Creed, the Lord's Prayer, and portions of the Order of Mass—texts that were also used in the Sunday gatherings of other Christians.[27] The work was continued by the International Consultation on English Texts, which in 1969 achieved substantial agreement for these and other texts among major Christian bodies.[28] By participating in these meetings, ICEL was contributing to the development of English-language worship among many ecclesial communities, and it was strengthening the bond among Christians by working together on texts for common prayer.

However, ICEL's efforts in this regard were discontinued after the publication of *Liturgiam authenticam*, which reflected a change of view on the relationship of liturgy and ecumenical dialogue. In time the CDWDS also recast the structure of ICEL through the approval of new statutes, by which ICEL no longer has a role in an ecumenical dialogue but focuses strictly on translation of liturgical books.

---

27 *New Catholic Encyclopedia*, 2nd ed. (Washington: Thomson-Gale, 2003), s.v. "Consultation on Common Texts."

28 *New Catholic Encyclopedia*, s.v. "International Consultation on English Texts."

## Authority

The question of the authority for translations was first addressed in *Sacrosanctum Concilium* (*Constitution on the Sacred Liturgy*), the first of the principal documents of the Second Vatican Council. There one reads that Latin is to be preserved, but since the vernacular "may frequently be of great advantage to the people, a wider use may be made of it."[29] The extent of the vernacular was to be determined by "competent territorial ecclesiastical authority,"[30] or the conferences of bishops.[31] The same authority—the territorial bishops' conference—was to approve the translations.[32] In truth, *Sacrosanctum Concilium* did not envision the complete use of the vernacular in the Mass. It called for the vernacular "in those parts which pertain to the people," who still should be able "to say or sing together in Latin those parts of the Ordinary of the Mass which pertain to them."[33] Still, it left open the possibility for more extended adaptations of the liturgy,[34] which was widely granted within a few years of the Council.

With *Liturgiam authenticam*, this authority shifted from local conferences of bishops to the Holy See:

> For the good of the faithful, the Holy See reserves to itself the right to prepare translations in any language, and to approve them for liturgical use. Nevertheless, even if the Apostolic See, by means of the Congregation for Divine Worship and the Discipline of the Sacraments, may intervene from time to time out of necessity in the preparation of translations, it still belongs to the competent Conference of Bishops to approve their assumption into liturgical use within the boundaries of a given ecclesiastical territory, unless otherwise explicitly indicated in the decree of approbation of the translation promulgated by the Apostolic See.

---

29  Second Vatican Council, *Sacrosanctum Concilium* (SC), no. 36:2, in *Vatican Council II: Volume 1: The Conciliar and Post Conciliar Documents*, ed. Austin Flannery (Northport, NY: Costello Publishing, 1996). Hereafter, Vatican II documents cited in this essay come from this edition.

30  SC, no. 36:3.

31  See SC, no. 22:2.

32  See SC, no. 36:4.

33  SC, no. 54.

34  See SC, no. 40.

Afterwards, for the purpose of obtaining the *recognitio* of the Holy See, the Conference shall transmit the decree of approbation for its territory together with the text itself, in accordance with the norms of this Instruction and of the other requirements of the law.[35]

Although local conferences of bishops continue to approve the translations in stages, the ultimate responsibility for them rests in the hands of the CDWDS in Rome.

# THE TRANSLATION OF THE THIRD EDITION OF THE *ROMAN MISSAL*

Two factors caused the coming of a new translation of the *Roman Missal*. One was the publication of the third edition in Latin; the other was the revised rules of translation. ICEL was charged with the project, and it set about this task through a process of broad consultation.

ICEL first considered the Order of Mass, as it had done when the *Missal* first went into English after the Second Vatican Council. The Order of Mass is a kind of script for every celebration of the Eucharist. Hence, it would be the most controversial part of the translation, and its completion would set the tone for the rest of the *Missal*. ICEL began with a base translation. The secretariat contacted an expert in the field to propose a good, usable translation following the norms of *Liturgiam authenticam*. A base translation is not an academic exercise, but a thoughtful proposal to put on the table for refinement. Other specialists in the field commented informally on the base translation of the Order of Mass, but the work was formally entrusted directly to the bishops of ICEL's commission. They labored over the working translation and proposed a revised text to their conferences of bishops. By the summer of 2008, nine of those conferences had voted in favor of the text, though some emendations were also proposed. The United States Conference of Catholic Bishops (USCCB) sent the Order of Mass to the CDWDS for its *recognitio* (approval), which the bishops obtained in the summer of 2008. The CDWDS made hundreds of changes—most of them rather small. For example, it capitalized the word "Priest" wherever it occurs; it introduced the word "brethren" as the first option where ICEL's translation has "brothers and sisters"; and

---

35 *Liturgiam authenticam*, no. 104.

in Eucharistic Prayer II it completely redrafted the first line following the Holy, Holy. The Order of Mass was thus the first section of the *Missal* to complete the long process from base translation to approval. Although the *recognitio* was given only for its use in the United States, few changes are expected when it is approved for other conferences of bishops. As *Liturgiam authenticam* states, "In the case of the Order of Mass and those parts of the Sacred Liturgy that call for the direct participation of the people, a single translation should exist in a given language, unless a different provision is made in individual cases."[36]

ICEL divided the rest of the *Missal* into about a dozen different parts and assigned each to a base translator. Most of the book is a collection of presidential prayers: that is, the collect, prayer over the offerings, and prayer after communion assigned for a given Mass formula, whether a Sunday in Advent or a saint's day in Ordinary Time. A base translation of all those prayers was prepared and shared with nine review teams, who commented on the work for its fidelity and suitability for public worship. These teams had other tools at their disposal: the original Latin text, source notes, and the 1998 translation proposed by ICEL prior to the changes of *Liturgiam authenticam*. In this way, the extensive work of the 1980s and 1990s was not abandoned. It served as a source of inspiration and analysis for those proposing the revision of the *Missal*. The resulting translation was called the "proposed text."

The proposed text from these nine different teams of translators was sent to a single body, the Roman Missal Editorial Committee (RMEC). This small international group of experts served as a funnel to receive all the work from the various translators and to unify the style and vocabulary.

At semi-annual meetings, ICEL's commission refined these texts. In attendance at a typical meeting have been the eleven bishops who make up the commission; three members of the secretariat from Washington, D.C.; the chair of the RMEC; and a few other invited experts and assistants. Seated at one table, the attendees took turns reading aloud one of the prayers under consideration. The chair, Bishop Arthur Roche of Leeds, England, invited comments. If changes were proposed, he put them to a vote of the members of the commission—not to others in attendance. The process moved rapidly but thoughtfully. Improvements to the texts

---

36 *Liturgiam authenticam*, no. 88.

happened at every meeting.

As the commission finished its work on one of the segments of the *Missal*, it voted on binding the results into a proposed translation called the "green book"—named after the color of the cover to be placed on the resulting manuscript. ICEL then sent its green books to the episcopal conferences for their comments. The conferences submitted suggested improvements back to the secretariat, which evaluated them and incorporated them into the next round of discussion among the bishops of the commission.

Once again, the commission and some associates met to review the texts, this time with suggested improvements to the green book. One by one the prayers were proclaimed aloud by participants, who then engaged in discussion about the improvements. If changes were made, they were voted upon prayer by prayer. At the conclusion of this stage, the bishops of the commission voted on the book again. If the revisions were approved as a unit, the work was now called a "gray book"—again denoting the color of the cover for the revised manuscript.

The gray book of each section was then sent to the conferences of bishops around the world. At this stage, the conferences were expected merely to vote yes or no. If they wished to make further changes to the text, they could propose emendations when the work was submitted to the CDWDS for its *recognitio*.

In the summer of 2008, the USCCB voted against the gray book for the Proper of Seasons. The Conference recommended changes, and the book won approval by the bishops in the fall of the year.

Ultimately, all the segments of the *Missal* need to be approved by all the conferences of English-speaking bishops. Then the CDWDS needs to grant its *recognitio*; and as is evident from the Order of Mass, the CDWDS may make changes to the gray books as it grants its final approval.

In Rome, the CDWDS is assisted by its own advisory panel, Vox Clara.[37] This group, formed in 2002, makes recommendations on the English translations at the different stages of the process. No member of Vox Clara sits on ICEL, and no member of ICEL participates in the meetings of Vox Clara. Vox Clara and the CDWDS send recommendations to ICEL as the work is unfolding. ICEL replies. Some of the work of these two bodies is bound to overlap because

---

37 In English, "vox clara" means "clear voice." In the Latin edition of the *Liturgy of the Hours*, the Sunday hymn for Advent morning prayer opens with these two words, a reference to John the Baptist, whose clear voice announces the coming of Christ.

they are working at the same project: rendering the same Latin texts into serviceable English. But the distinction of the two bodies pertains primarily to their range of authority. ICEL can be viewed as an arm of the English-speaking conferences of bishops, Vox Clara as an arm of the CDWDS. According to *Liturgiam authenticam*, the CDWDS holds the final authority over the vernacular translations, so Vox Clara, which has no authority of its own, still finds itself in an influential position. There is no parallel to Vox Clara in any other language group. The CDWDS has asked for this kind of assistance only for English translations.[38]

The pope is also involved in the translation process, because some of the changes affect the words of consecration at the Mass—the sacramental formula. The CDWDS must submit such a change to the authority of the Supreme Pontiff.[39] Several changes to these words have now been approved in the revised Order of Mass. For example, under the second edition of the *Roman Missal*, the priest says, "Take this, all of you, and drink from it: this is the cup of my blood, the blood of the new and everlasting covenant. It will be shed for you and for all so that sins may be forgiven." But using the revised translation expected to appear in the *Roman Missal*, Third Edition, the priest will say, "Take this, all of you, and drink from it, for this is the chalice of my blood, the blood of the new and eternal covenant, which will be shed for you and for many for the forgiveness of sins." Only the pope can approve such a change.

# STYLES OF THE VERNACULAR

All of this is bringing about a different style of the vernacular. It will call for a change in the way the texts are proclaimed as well as the way they are heard.

Most notable will be the length of sentences. The present English translation broke up long Latin sentences into two or three independent clauses. This has made the content easier to grasp, but it has caused some meaning to be lost. It also introduced a style of prayer in which the Church makes statements to God about what

---

38  At this writing, the committee is chaired by Cardinal George Pell of Sydney, Australia. The first vice-chairman is the Archbishop Emeritus Oscar Lipscomb of Mobile. The secretary is Archbishop (Emeritus) Alfred Hughes of New Orleans. The treasurer is Cardinal Justin Rigali of Philadelphia (*Newsletter: Committee on Divine Worship*, vol. 44 [May-June 2008]: 19).

39  See *Liturgiam authenticam*, no. 85.

God should already know, so the link between the address of the divinity and the request of the prayer has been broken. Longer sentences that retain the subordination of clauses will make the content richer, but they do call for more careful proclamation and hearing. Still, the longer sentences have been in use in the vernacular translations of other modern languages. English speakers should be able to grasp the meaning of longer clauses just as well as speakers of French or Spanish do.

The texts in the new translation are in a higher linguistic register. They are slightly more formal than those in the previous translation. They presume a stylized liturgy and an educated assembly. The disparity between God and the assembly will be stressed, for the texts assume a more submissive stance before the power of the divinity. Words that affirm God's mercy, expressions that denote the unworthiness of those speaking, and the expression "we pray" appear frequently in the newly translated prayers to punctuate the sentences with a reminder of the boldness implicit in any address directed to God.

The vocabulary of the third edition is broader. The current translation used a fairly narrow range of words to render the wide variety of the *Missal's* lexicon. The broader English vocabulary in the new translation is meant to honor the content of the *editio typica* but also to add variety to the expressions used in prayer.

The third edition presents rubrics with a more consistent vocabulary and style. Many of the rubrics have been updated to reflect the experience of the Church in praying the revised liturgy. Care is being made to make the translations of certain terms and phrases uniform throughout the *Missal* and other books.

The new translations are being made with an ear for singing. Many of the new texts will be sung, and the rhythms and words need a melodious foundation. ICEL has a special committee working on the chants for the new *Missal,* and its work should show how singable the new translation has become.

The alternative opening prayers found in the current Sacramentary were composed as paraphrases of the Latin text. However, in accordance with the principles of *Liturgiam authenticam,* the third edition of the *Roman Missal* will offer only an accurate translation of the collect for each Mass.

There is no change to the parts of the Mass where the priest or deacon uses "these or similar words." But the implication is that the words will be few, carefully chosen, and in harmony with the other words of the Mass.[40]

# WHY A NEW TRANSLATION?

One of the most frequently asked questions is, Why are we getting a new translation? There are various reasons, but most important is that the Church is in a good position now to improve the translation and that, after forty years of use, the time has come to freshen the texts. The revised translation will have a different style and vocabulary, which for some worshipers will require a period of adjustment; but in time the work will bear the intended fruit.

Several factors make a new translation opportune. Translators have a better insight now into the meaning of the original texts, and a better sense of what sounds right when it is proclaimed aloud. A style that more closely imitates the Latin structures will reflect the formality of the liturgy and the seriousness with which the faithful approach it. The translation can also better harmonize the English words with those of other language groups. The entire Church will be praying with a more unified voice. All of these factors should help the Church divine the vernacular.

The most obvious answer to the question "Why are we getting a new translation?" is "To make it resemble the Latin more accurately." But this reason will puzzle many English speakers, especially those who know only one language. Americans have a global reputation for having a poor facility with any language other than English, and the reputation is justly deserved. Many Americans do not appreciate the value of reading Dante in Italian or Rilke in German. They sponsor English-only legislation to minimize the voice of other languages in state after state. Given this cultural background, it is no surprise that Americans wonder why it is so important to have a *Missal* that resembles its original language. But the Latin texts are the fruit of many centuries of theological reflection and pastoral experience. They carefully nuance the faith of the Church. Many of them are

---

40    See GIRM, no. 31.

beautiful and eloquent. To use a vernacular that adheres more closely to the Latin will give a clearer voice to the Church's faith.

Many people have contributed to the translations. The base translators, the review teams, the RMEC, the ICEL secretariat, the ICEL commission, the conferences of bishops, Vox Clara, the CDWDS, and even the pope have all put their fingerprints on the texts. Some might argue that too many people have contributed to the project, but it is better to have too many than too few.

Once the texts are published, if history is any guide, they will be subject to great criticism. As with any work of this magnitude, the new texts will have strengths and weaknesses. Overall, though, it is hoped that the new translation will mark an improvement over the one currently in use, and that it will assist future generations of worshipers to lift mind and heart to God in prayer.

# About the Authors

**Most Reverend Gerald F. Kicanas** ("Liturgical Leadership in a Time of Change") is bishop of Tucson, Arizona. Ordained a priest for the Archdiocese of Chicago in 1967, he served in various capacities in the Archdiocese's seminary system for more than 25 years. Bishop Kicanas holds a PhD in educational psychology and an M.Ed in guidance and counseling. Bishop Kicanas was elected vice president of the United States Conference of Catholic Bishops in 2007.

**Rev. John J. M. Foster, JCD** ("Liturgical Implementation of the *Roman Missal*"), is an assistant professor of canon law at the Catholic University of America in Washington, D.C. Ordained for the Diocese of Stockton, Fr. Foster earlier served his diocese as a pastor and director of the diocesan worship office.

**Very Reverend Mark Francis, CSV** ("Liturgical Participation of God's People"), holds a doctorate in sacred liturgy from the Pontifical Liturgical Institute of Sant'Anselmo in Rome. Currently superior general of his religious community, the Viatorians, Fr. Francis taught liturgy for twelve years at the Catholic Theological Union in Chicago and has also served on the revision and translation subcommittee of the International Commission on English in the Liturgy. Fr. Francis has written widely on liturgical topics and is especially interested in the relationship between liturgy and culture.

**Rev. Paul Turner** ("Divining the Vernacular of Ritual Texts") is pastor of St. Munchin parish in Cameron, Missouri, in the Diocese of Kansas City–St. Joseph. Holding a doctorate in sacred theology from Sant' Anselmo in Rome and author of several books on liturgical topics, he is a former president of the North American Academy of Liturgy. He has served as a translator for the International Commission on English in the Liturgy.